Santa's Coming

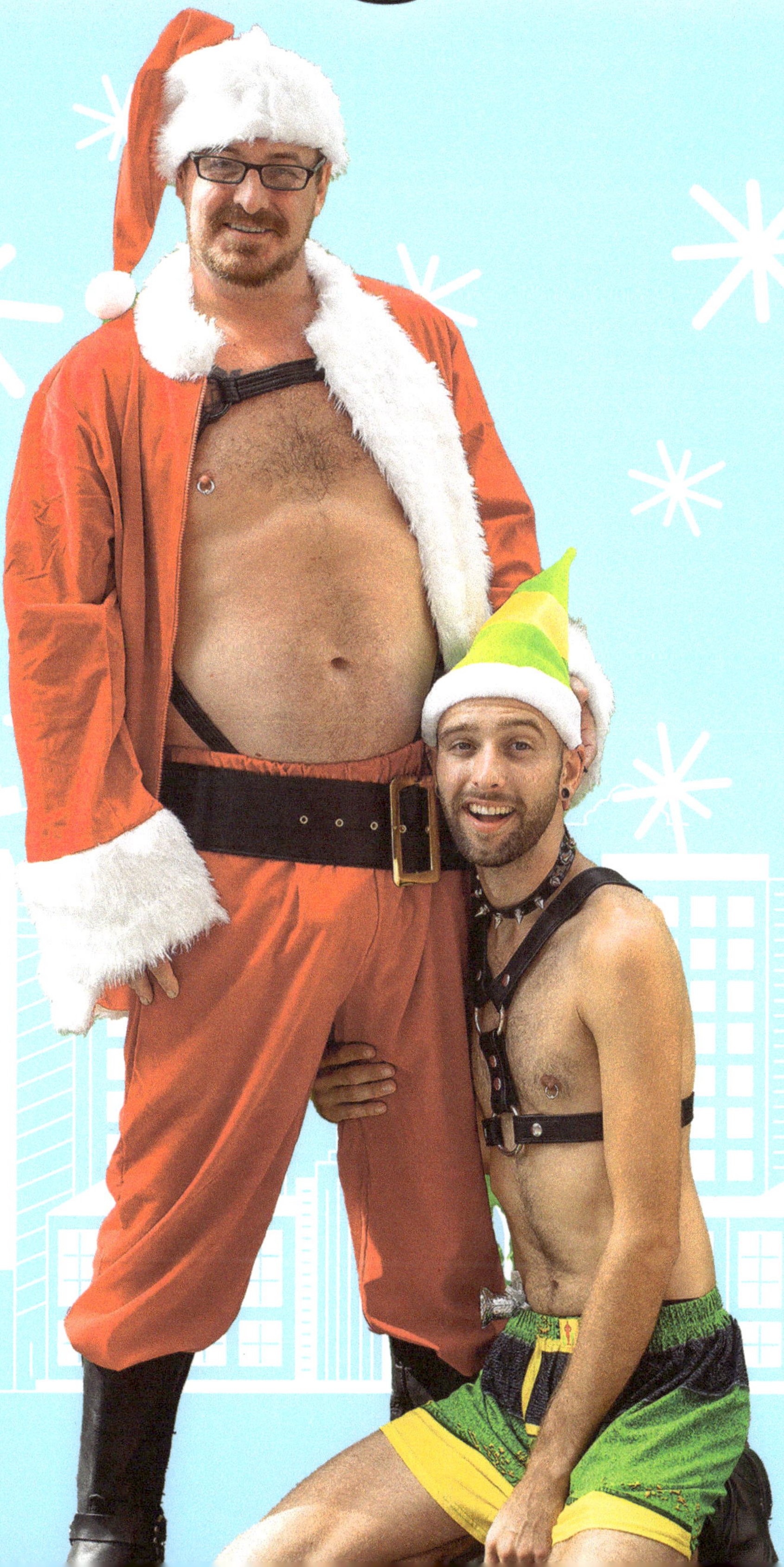

by Elizabeth Barkley

Photo credits:

Blu Velvet Photography, Fort Worth, Texas
Brandon Holmes Photography, Houston, Texas
Justin Oldmixon Photography, Austin, Texas

Contributors:
Austin Puppy Culture, a club organized to promote puppy culture, provide information, support, and social connection for Austin area pups, handlers, and allies. All LGBTQ+ pets are welcome.

Bayou City Pups, a nonprofit organization, a pack, that provides an outlet for social, recreational, and educational activities among adults of like mind: pups, handlers, and supporters.

Cecilia Urban, an aspiring illustrator and writer.

San Antonio Kennel Klub (SAKK Pack), a 501(c)(3) established in 2021 as a common home for San Antonio area pups, handlers, pup culture enthusiasts, and allies. The organization's mission is aimed at inclusion, community visibility, education of pup culture, and fundraising for other LGBTQIA+ causes/efforts and nonprofits.

Sir Rat Leather and Gear, a gay-owned and gay-operated clothing and entertainment store with convenient locations in Austin and Houston, Texas. They craft handmade leather and fetish clothing and offer it at affordable prices. They give back to the LGBTQ+ community by supporting local charities, artists, and organizations.

ISBN: 979-8-9851739-0-1 (sc)
ISBN: 979-8-9851739-1-8 (d)
ISBN: 979-8-9851739-4-9 (h)

Published June 2022

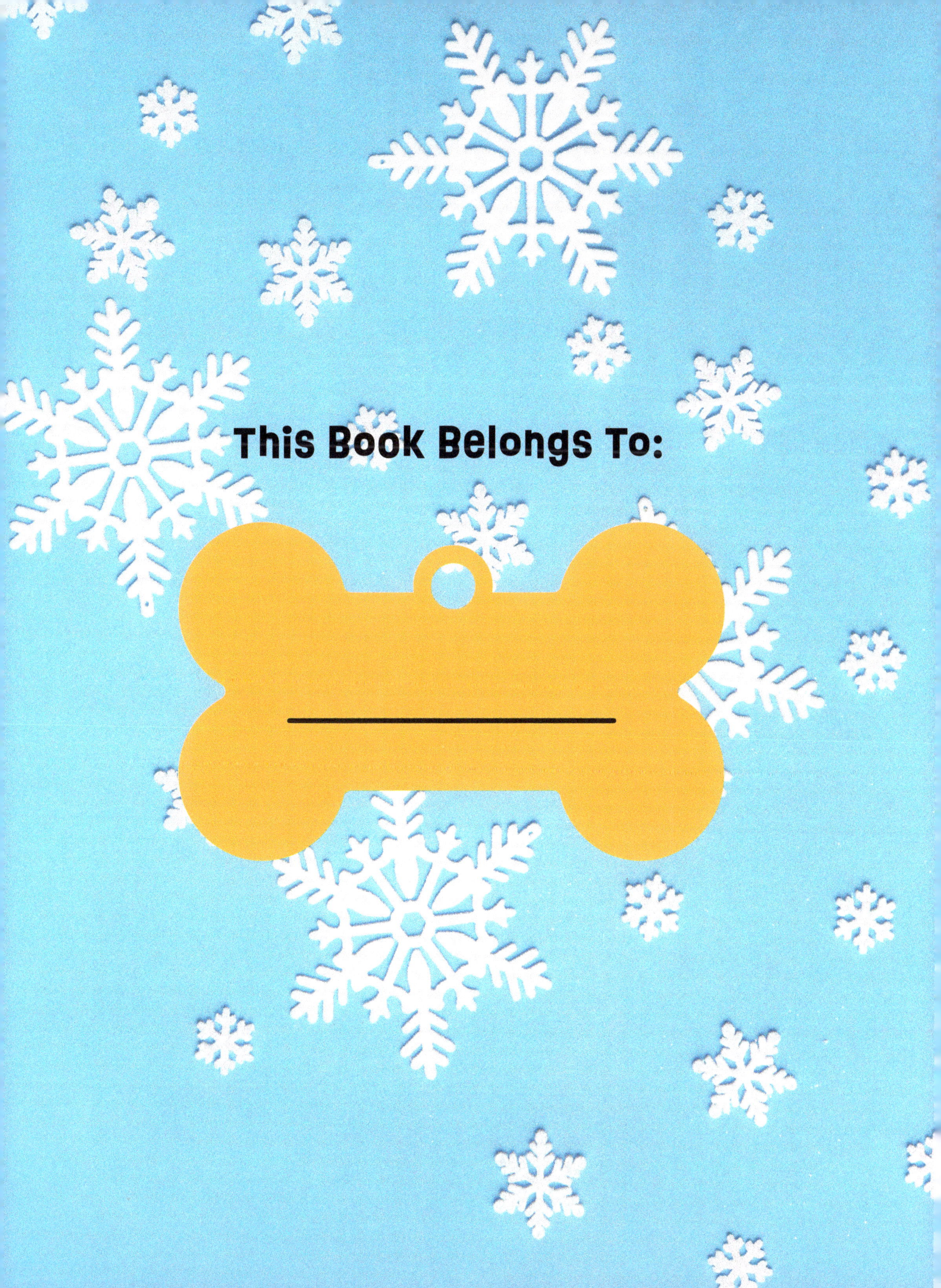
This Book Belongs To:

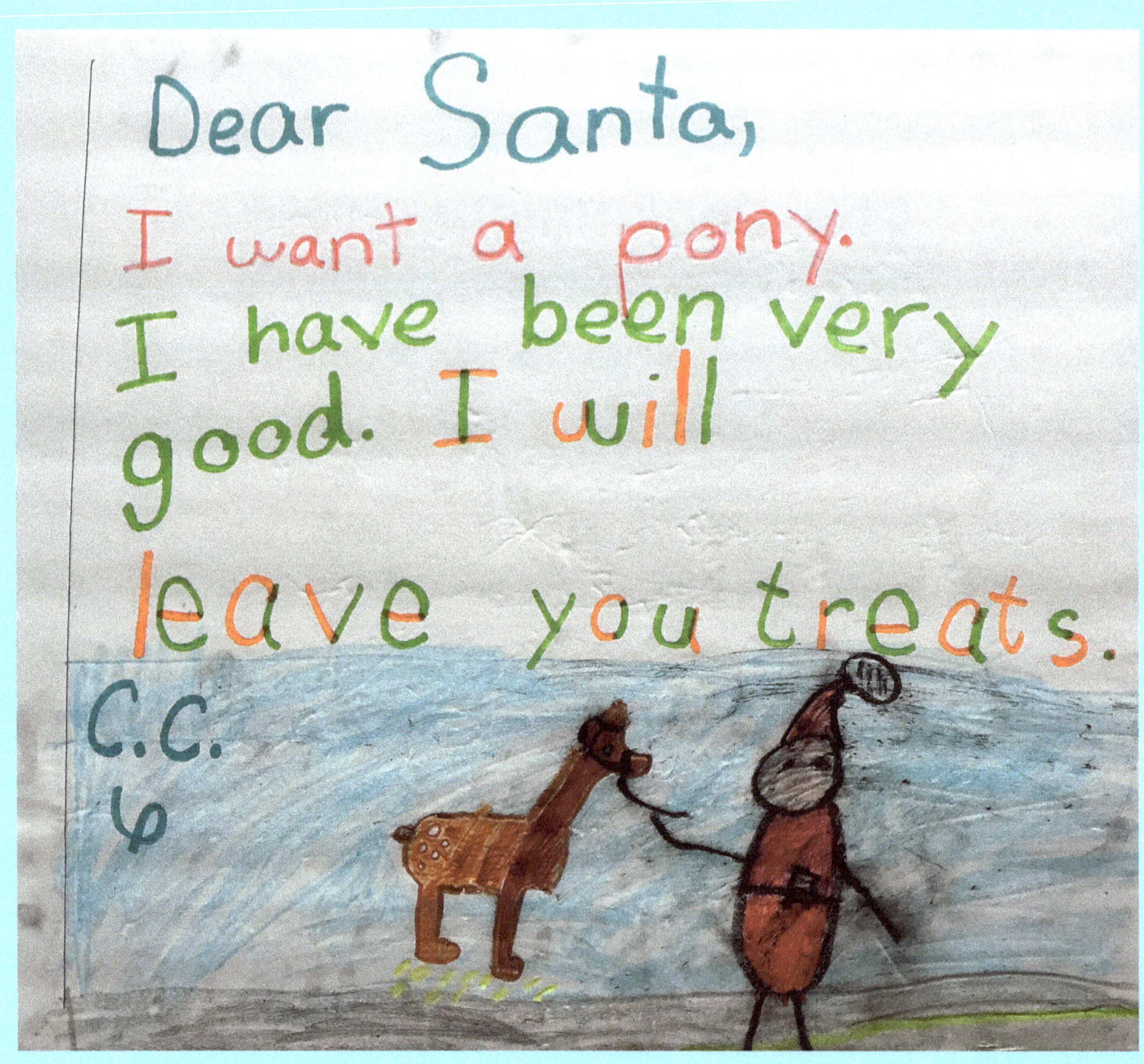
Dear Santa,
I want a pony.
I have been very
good. I will
leave you treats.
C.C.
6

He doesn't think twice about rewarding the nice.

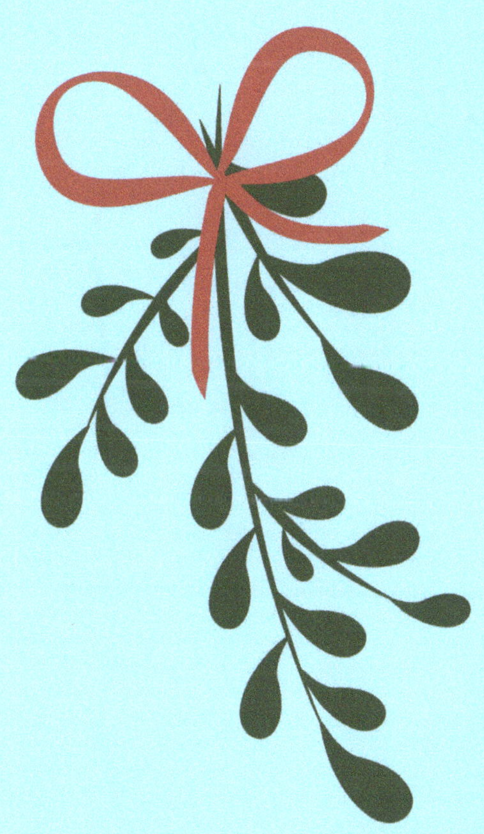

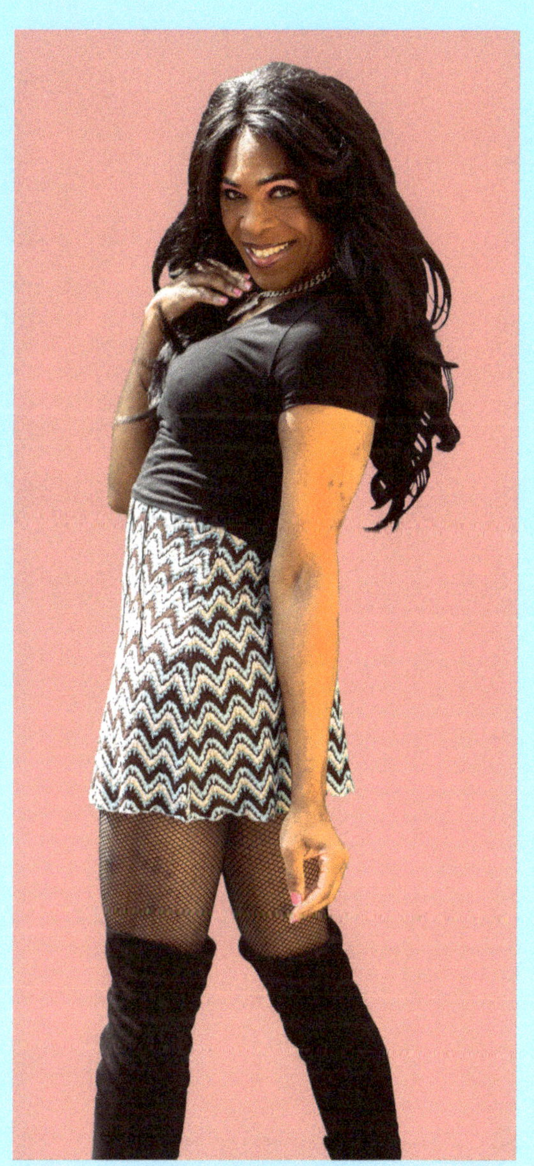

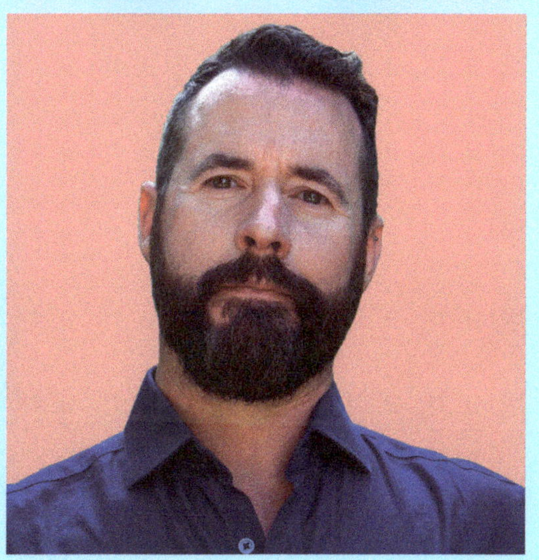

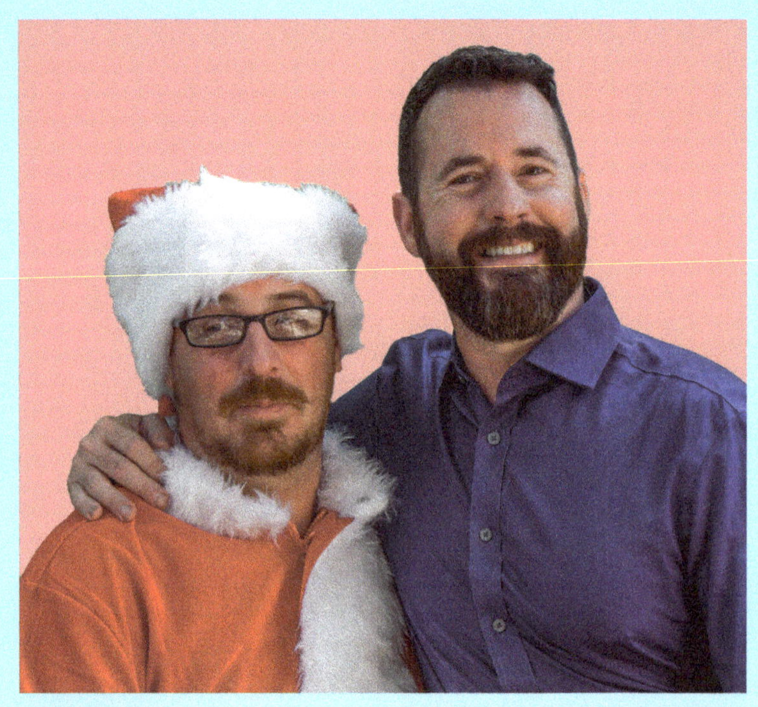

And why should he?
Nice is...nice.

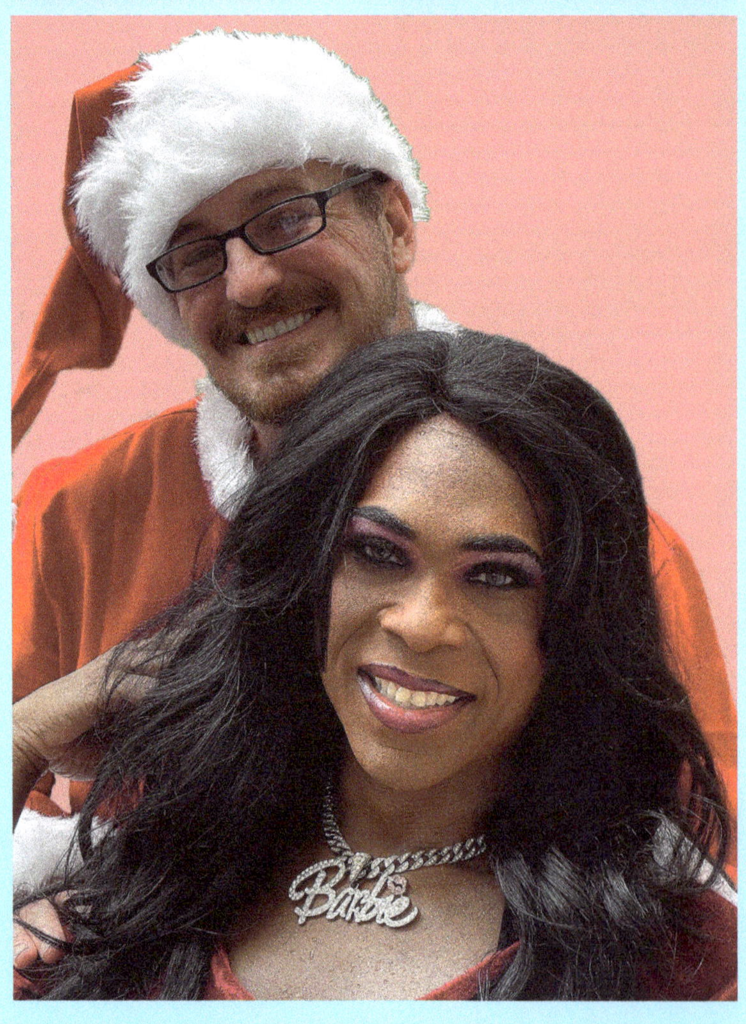

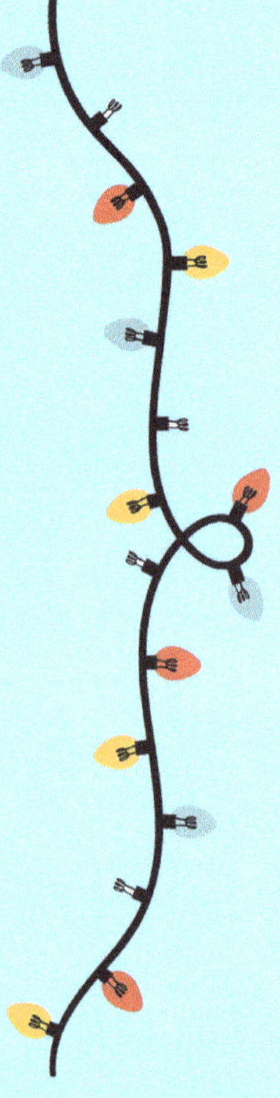

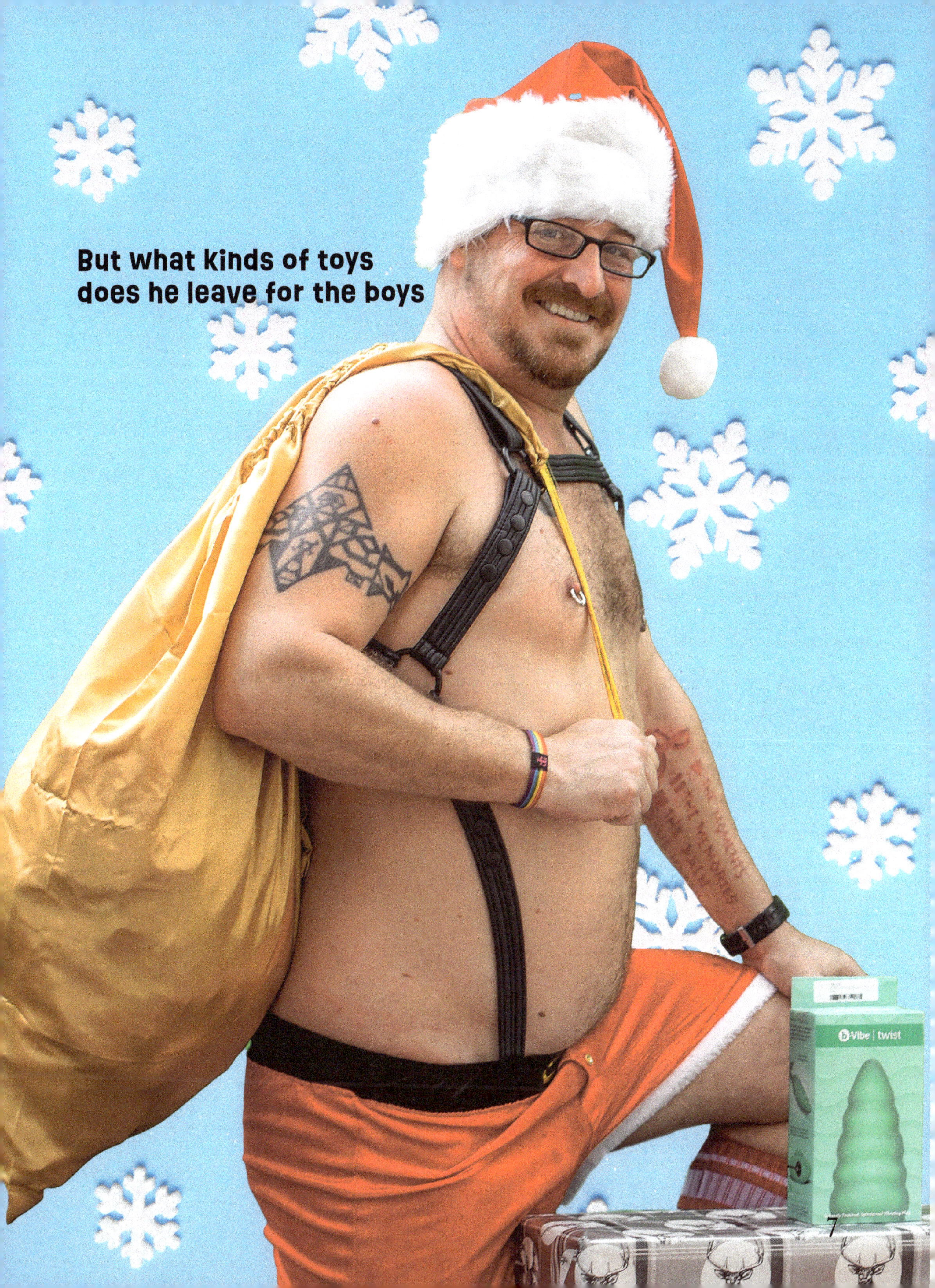
But what kinds of toys
does he leave for the boys
b-Vibe | twist

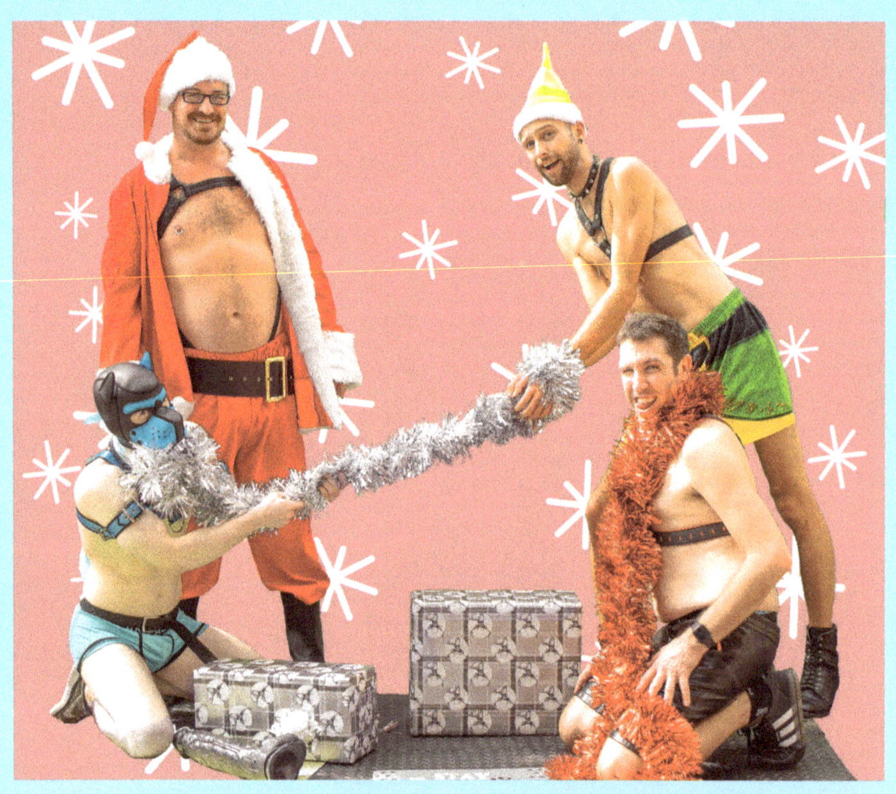

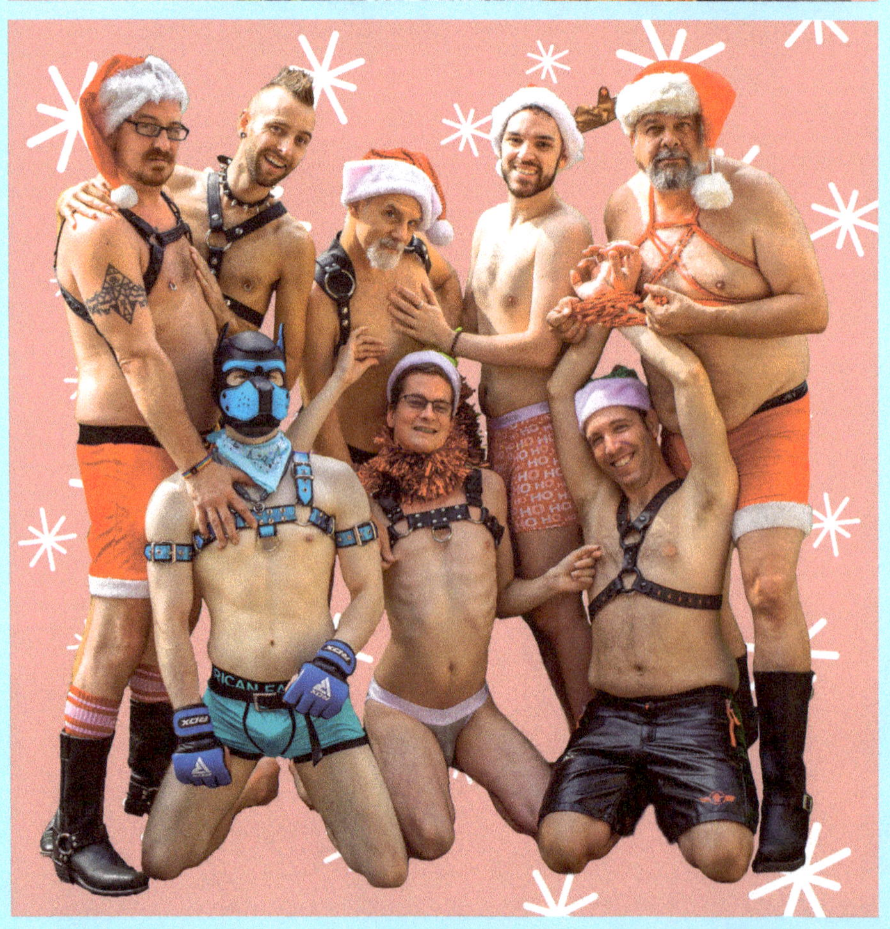

**who sparkle
and shine
and get out
of line?**

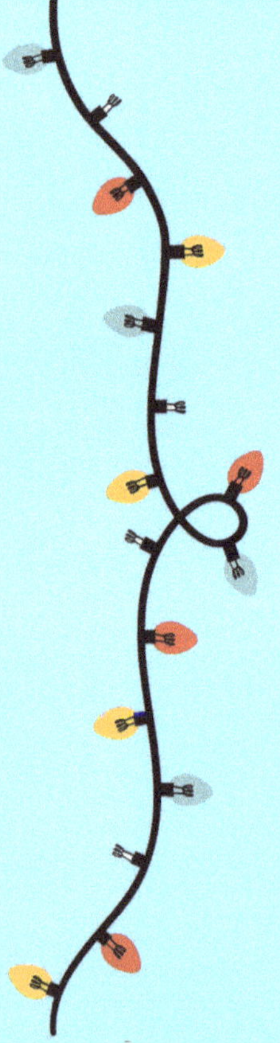

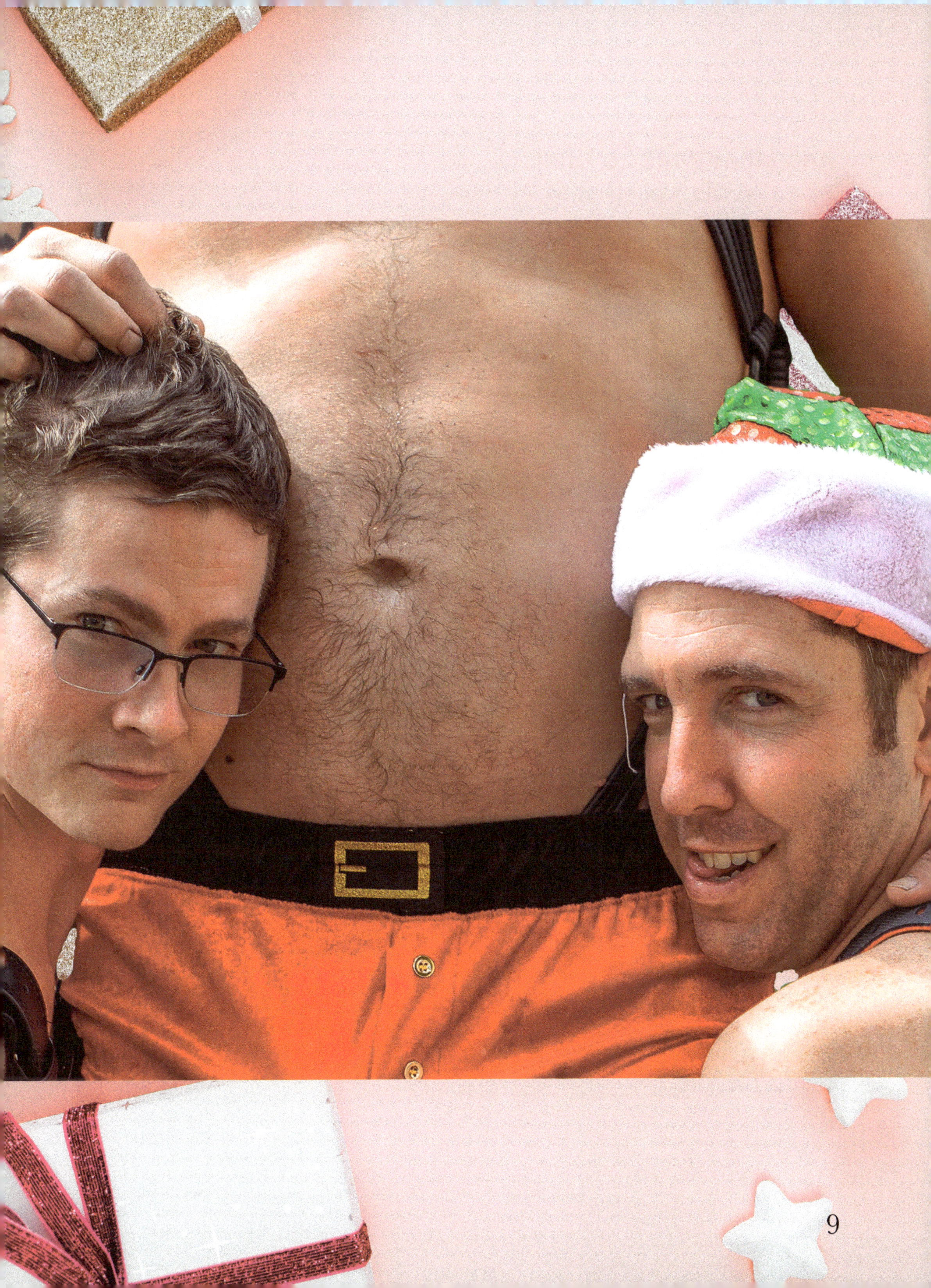

And what does he think about a diva with slink?

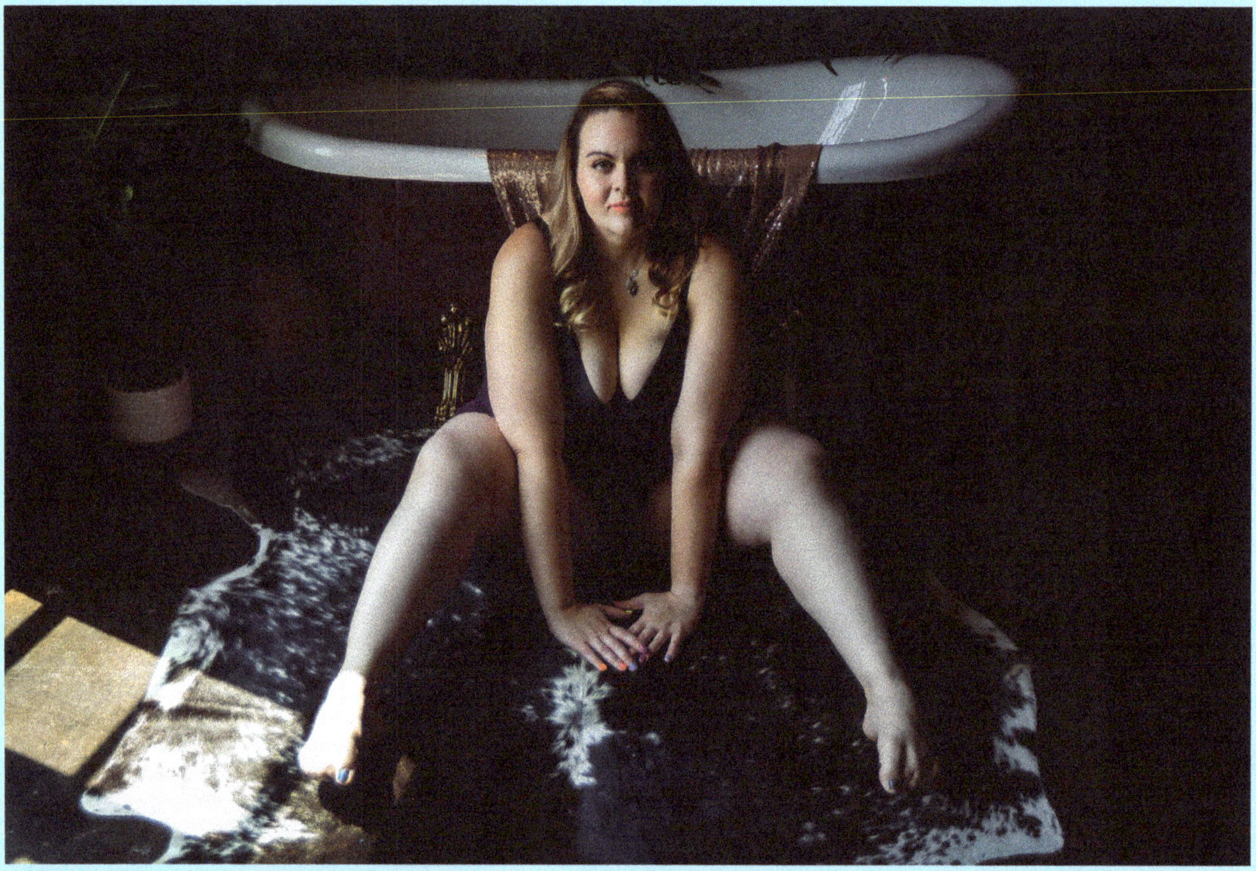

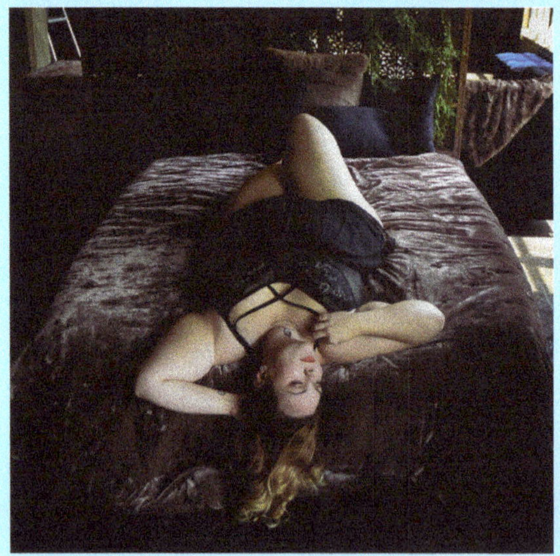

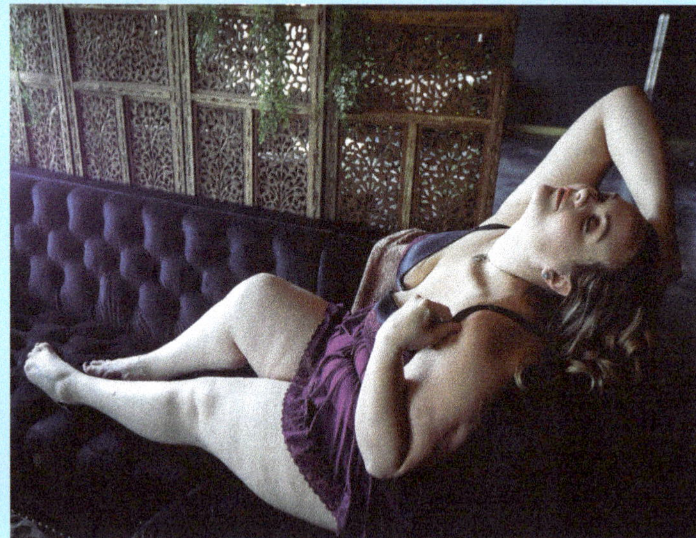

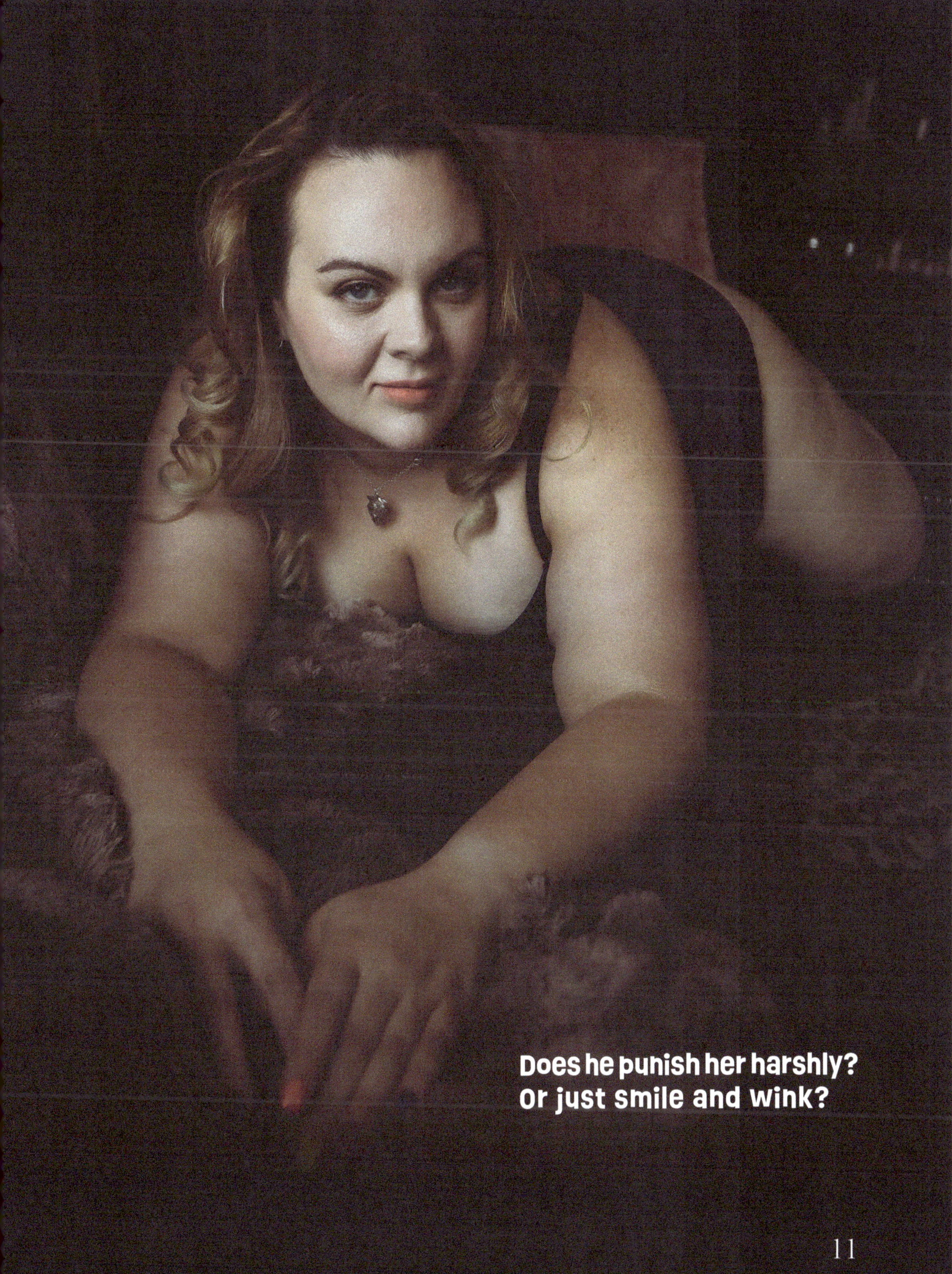
Does he punish her harshly?
Or just smile and wink?

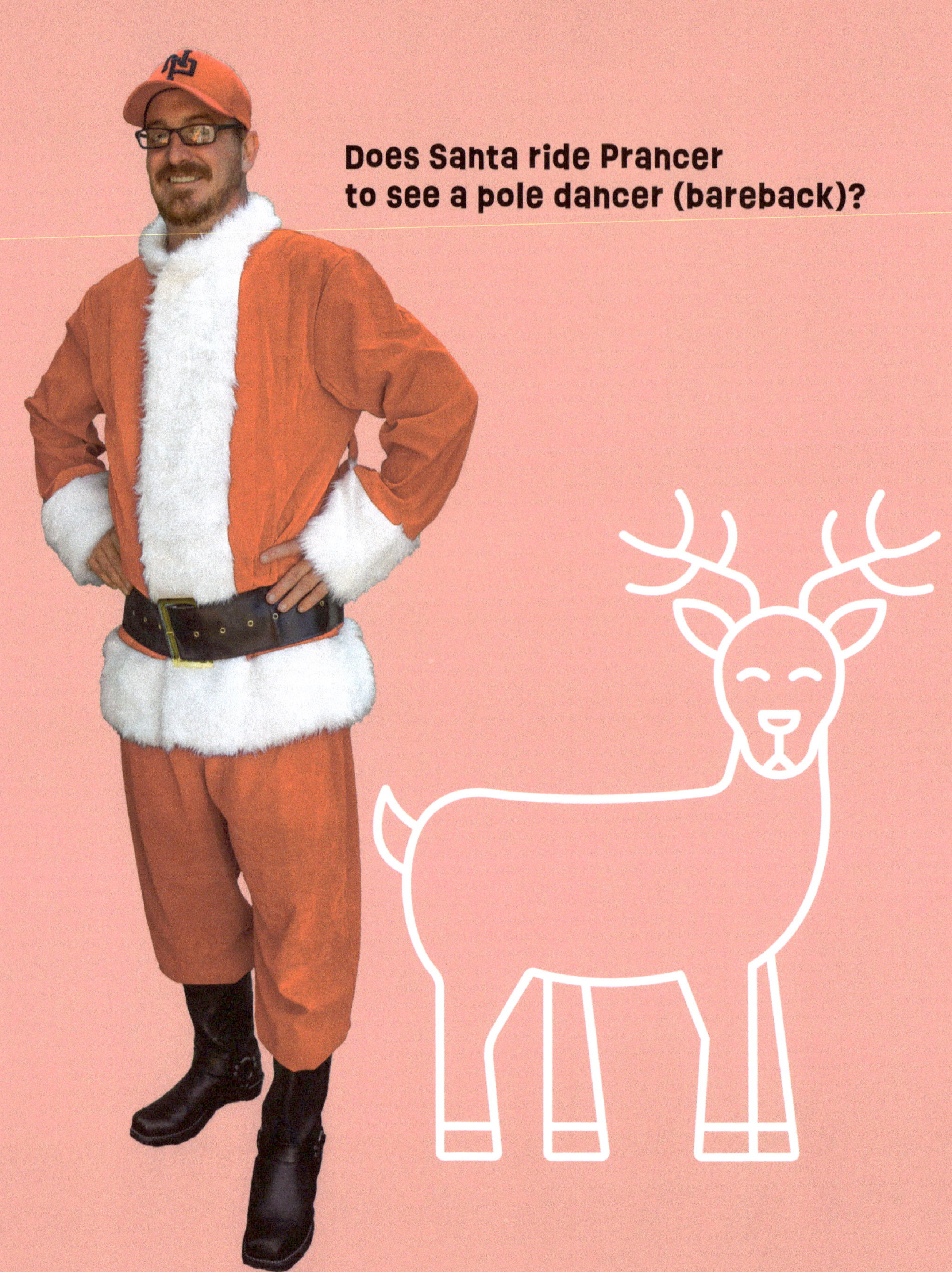

**Does Santa ride Prancer
to see a pole dancer (bareback)?**

Or does he make his way with a ride in his sleigh?

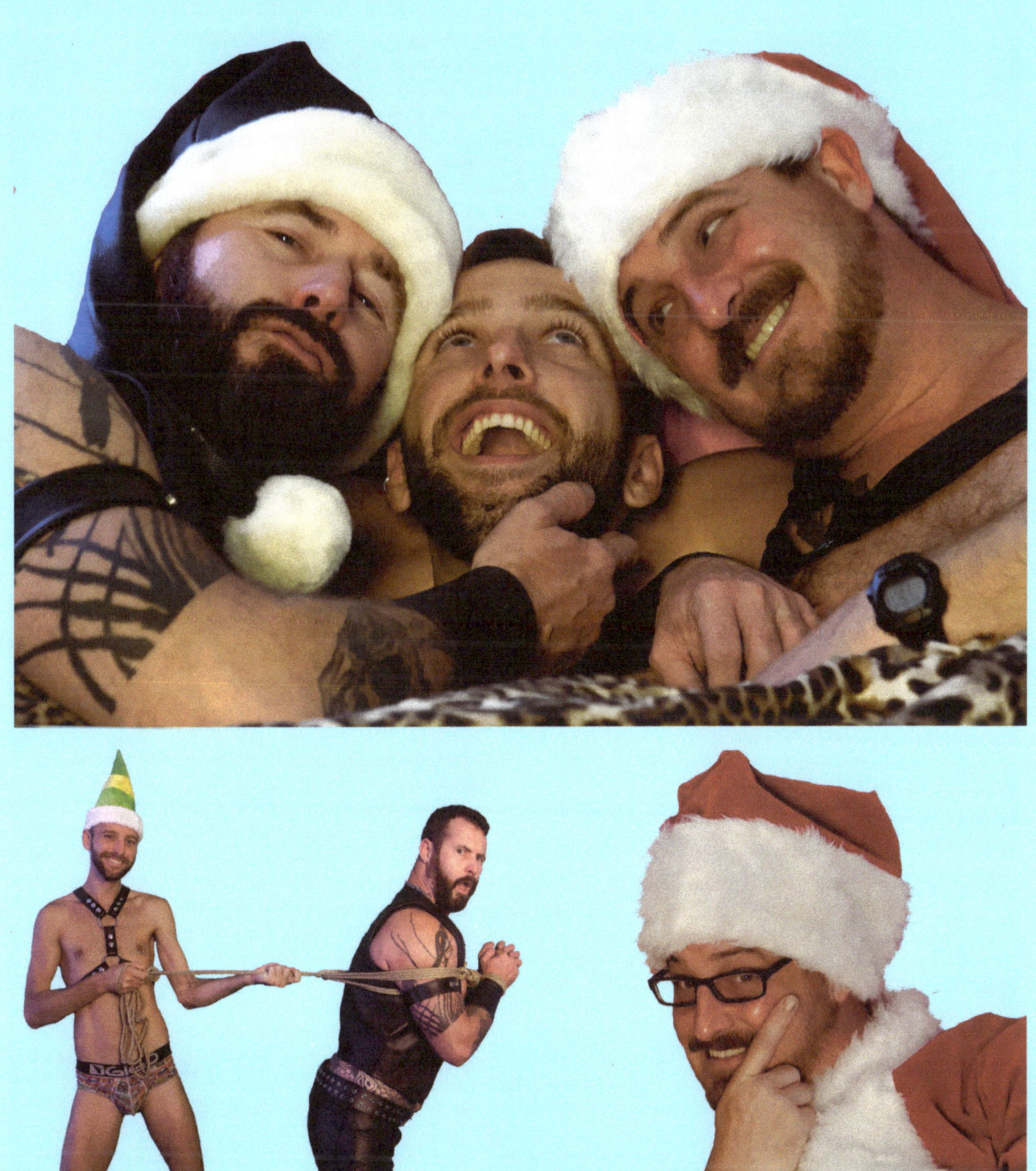

With what does he lavish the shameless

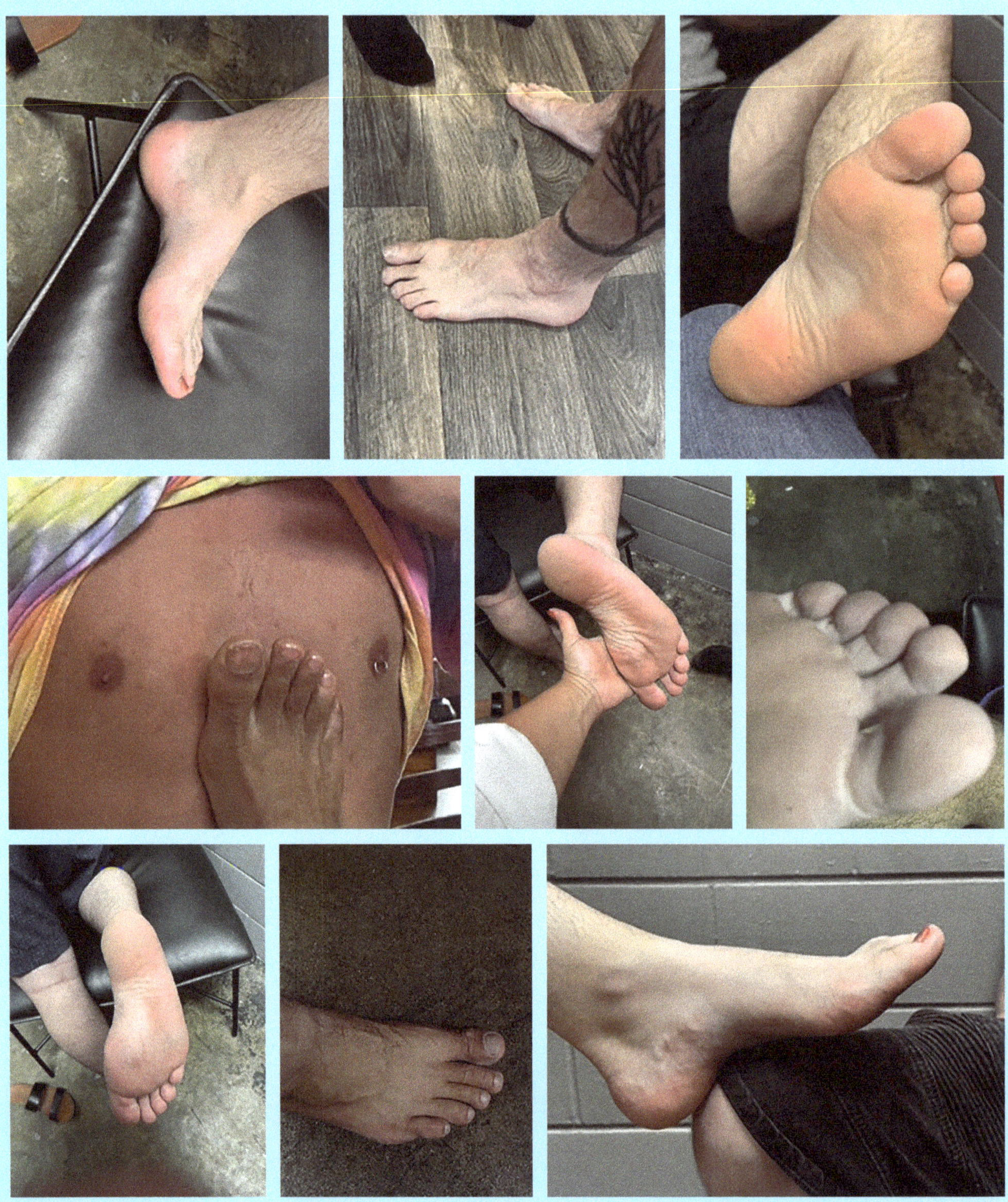

who ravish
pretty toes with nails painted?

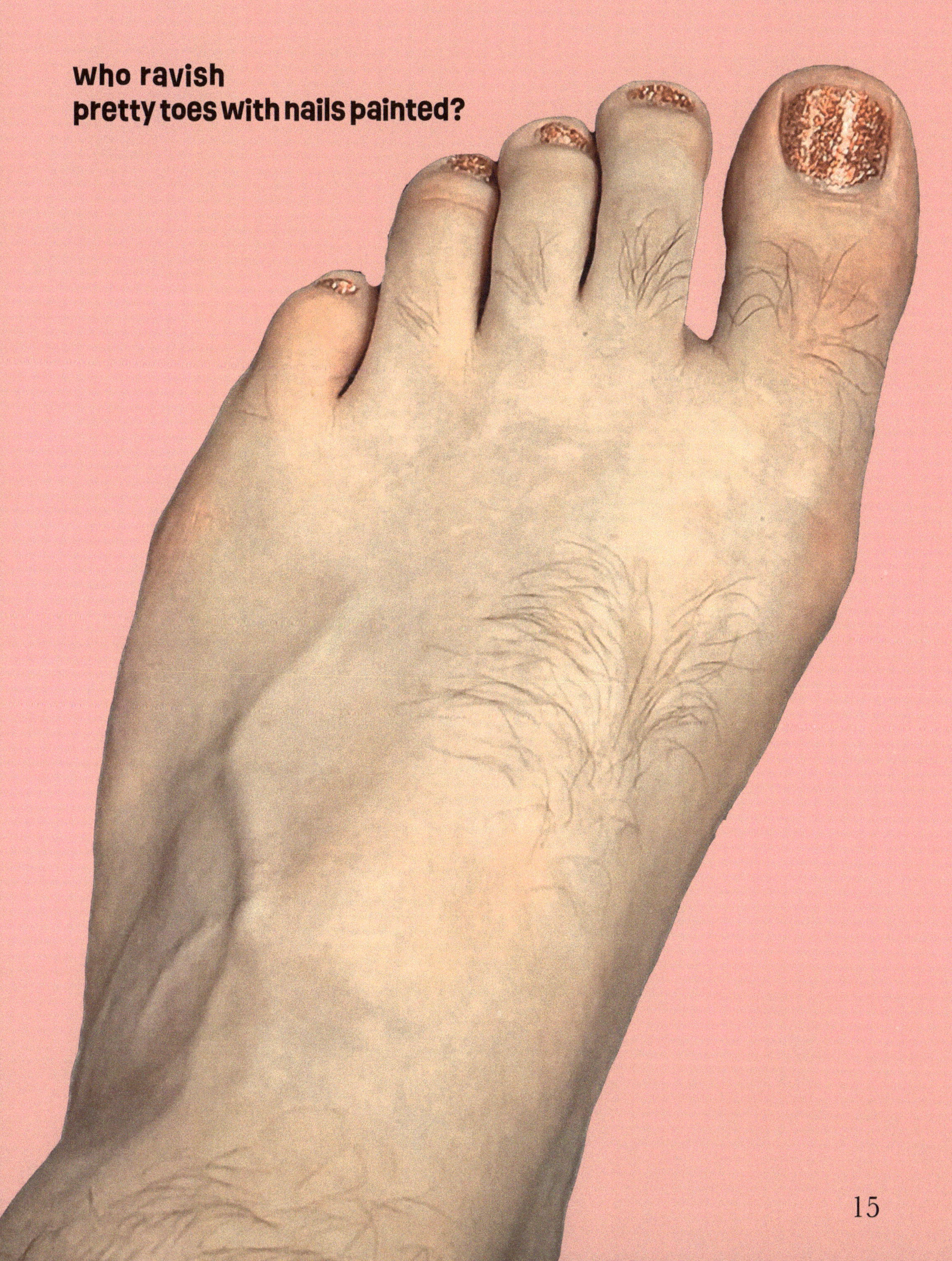

Does Santa bring booty to each little cutie?

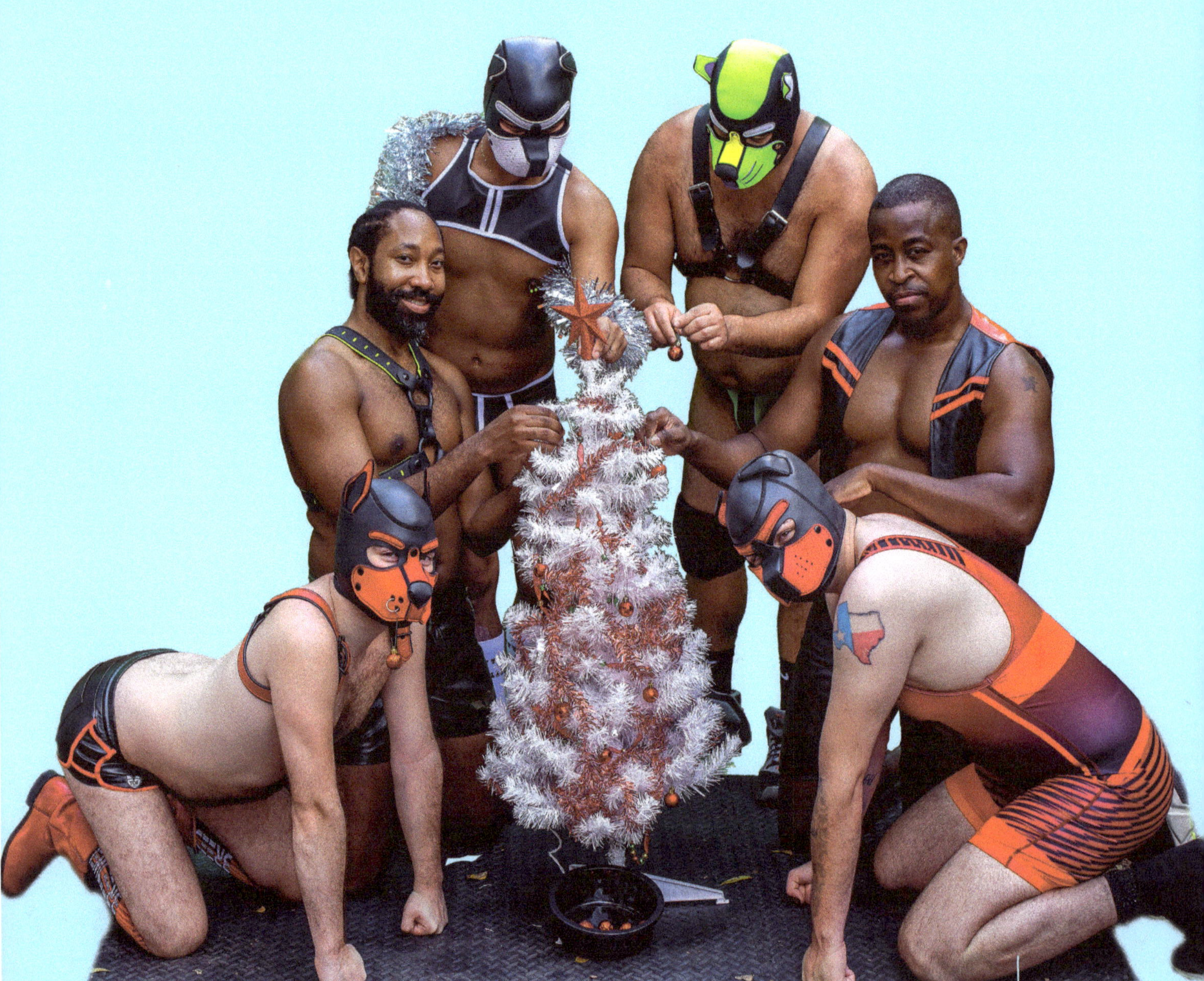

Or does he fill stockings with switches and coal?

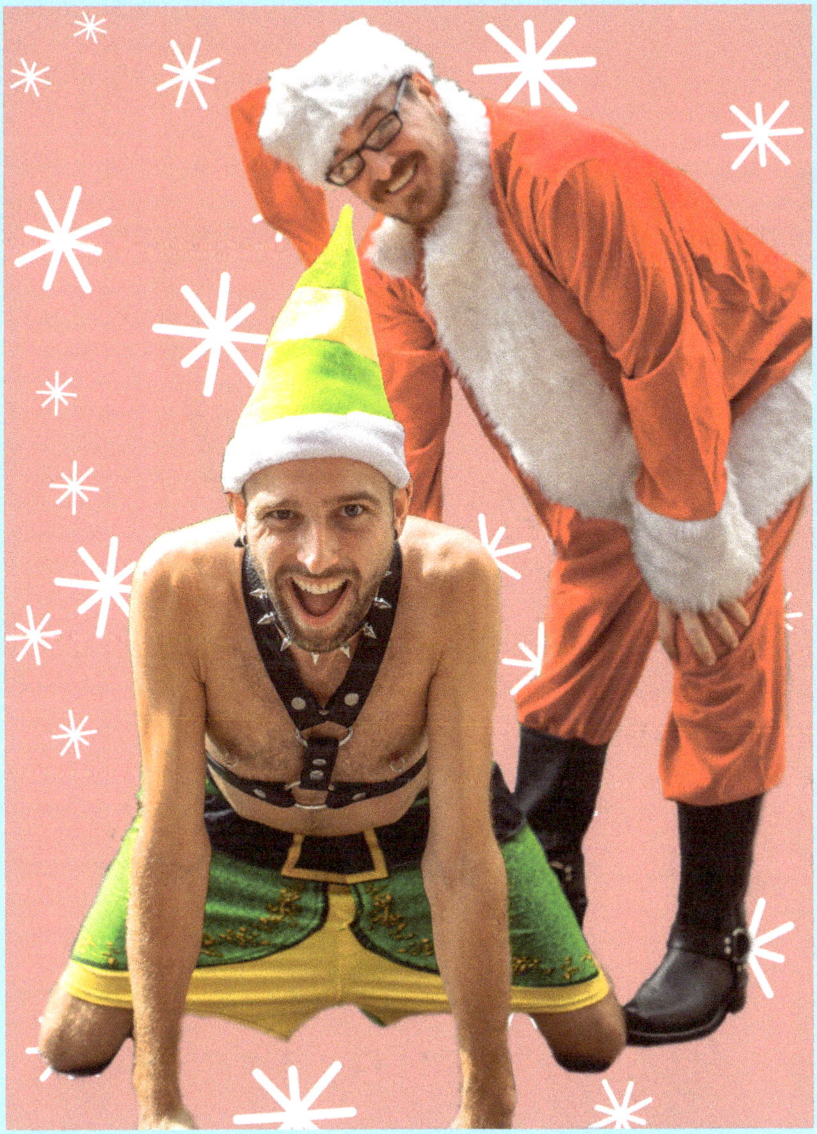

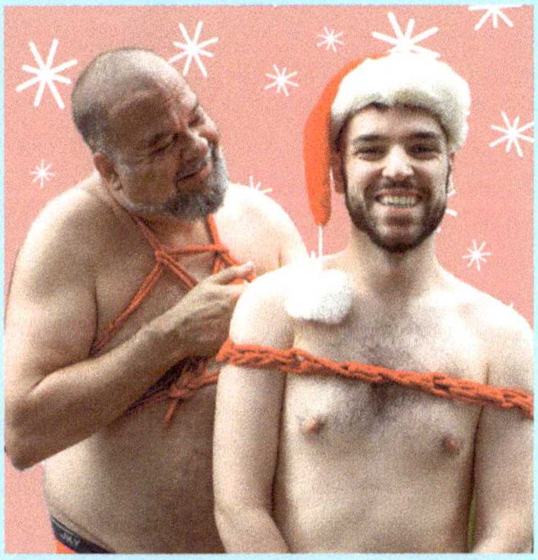

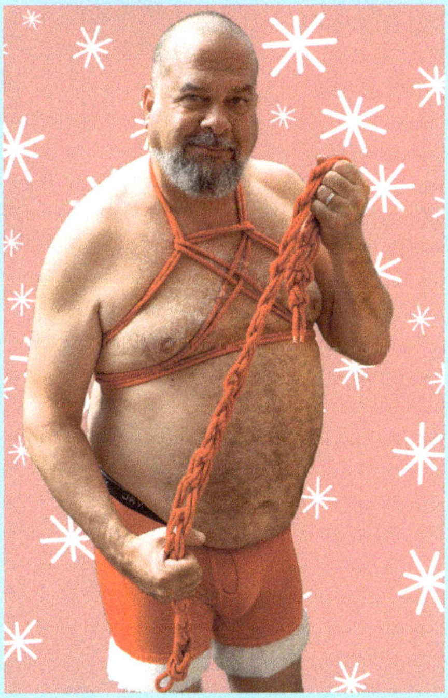

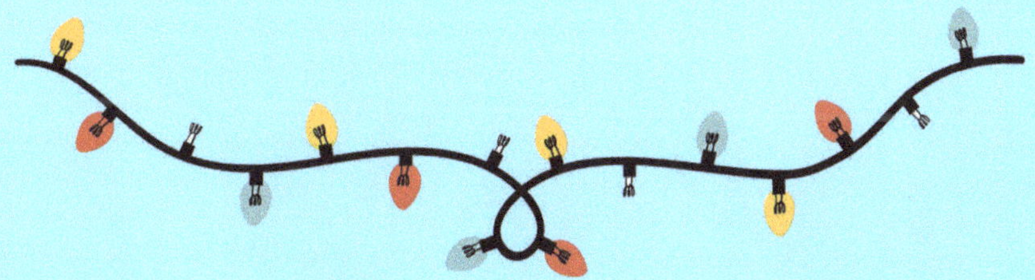

What does it matter on the North Pole

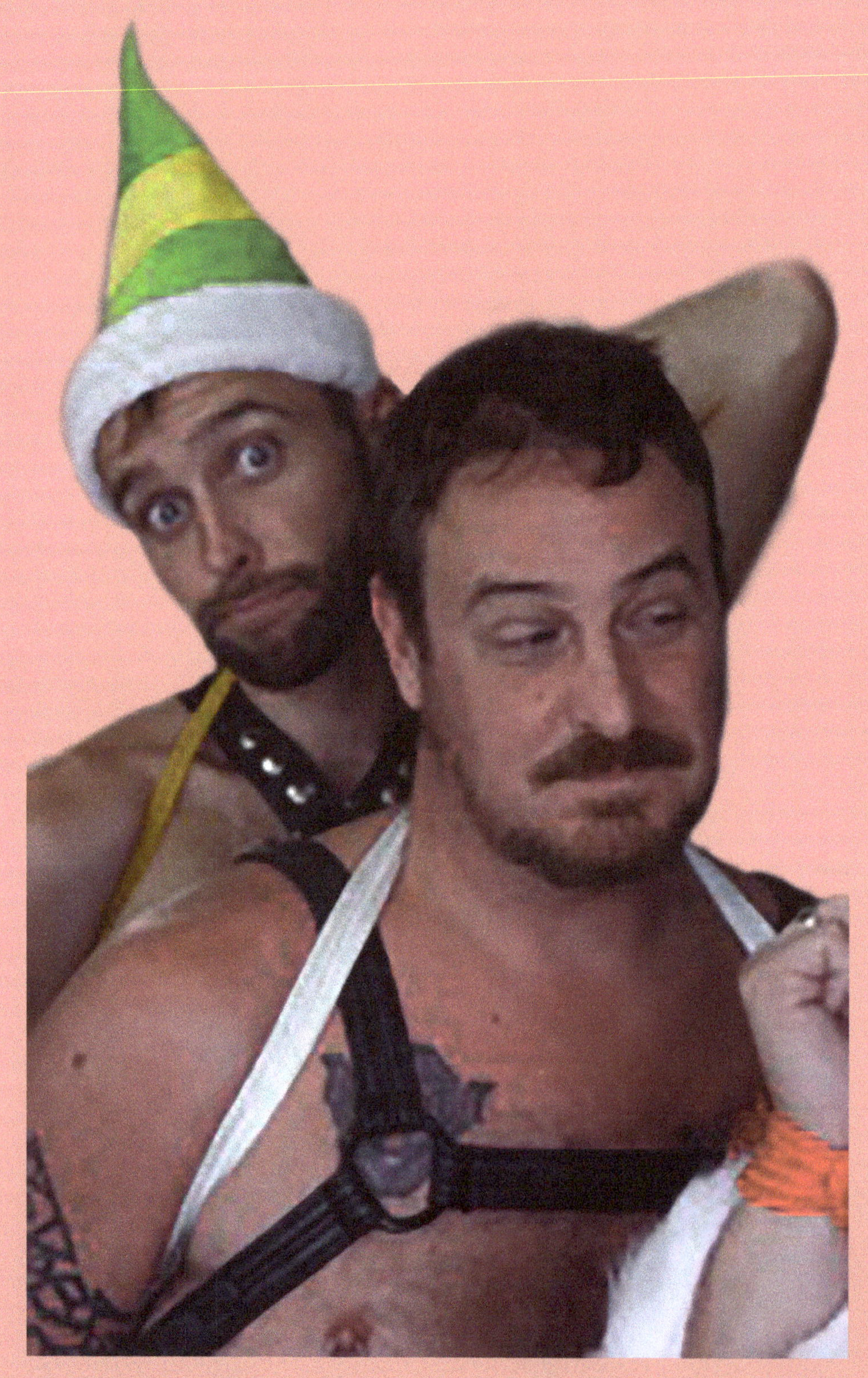

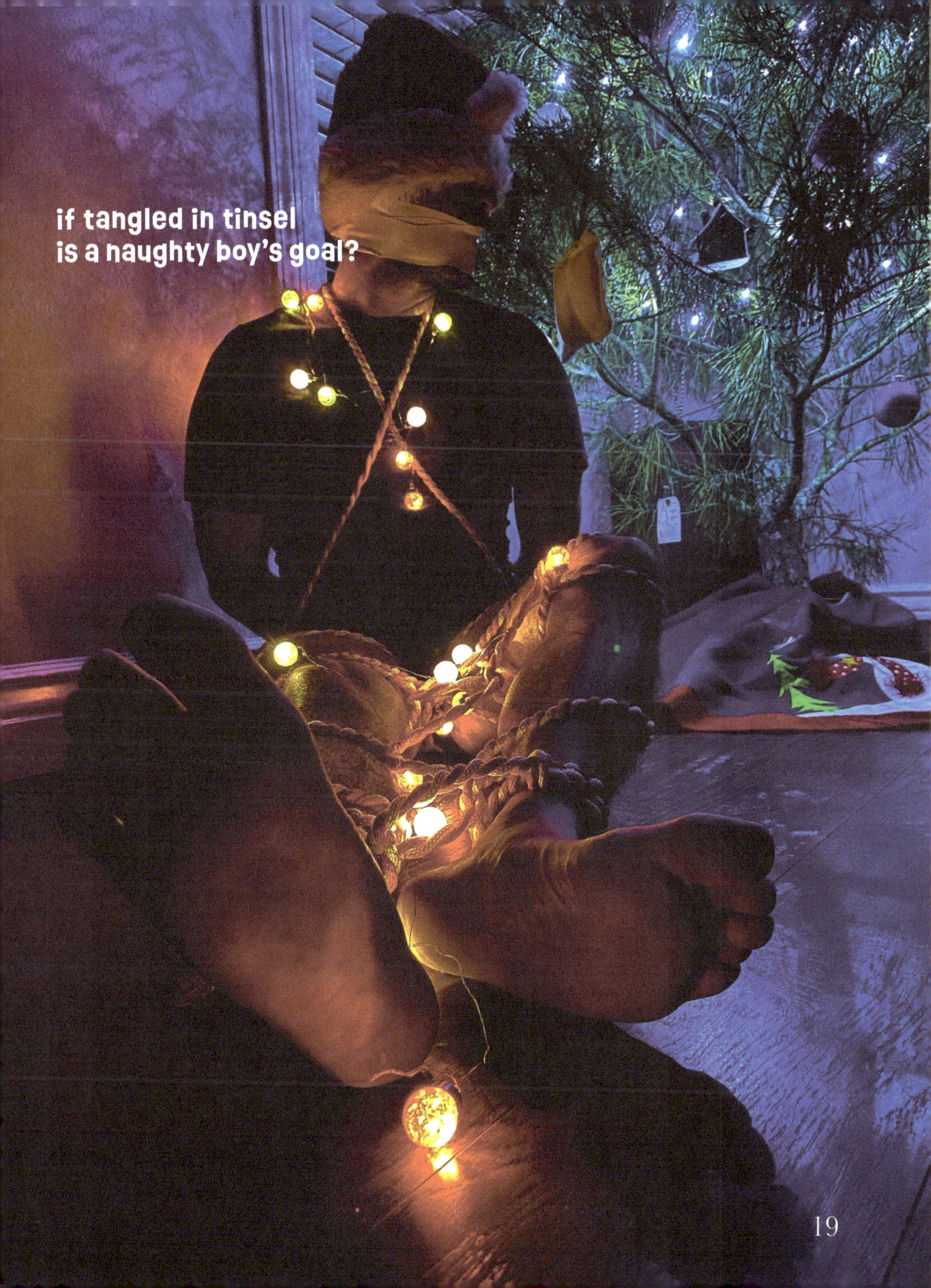
if tangled in tinsel
is a naughty boy's goal?

Wouldn't you like to know

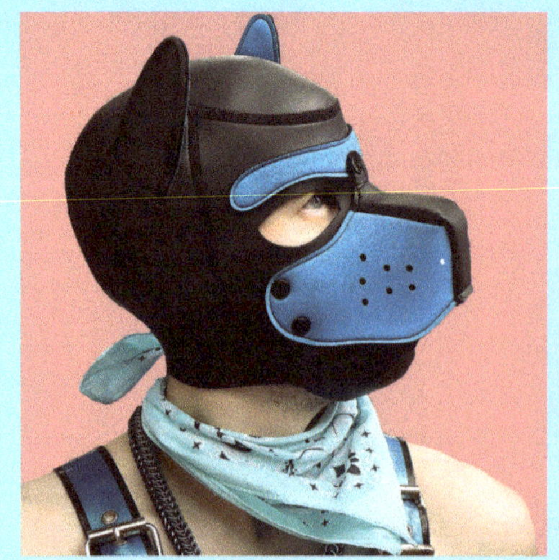

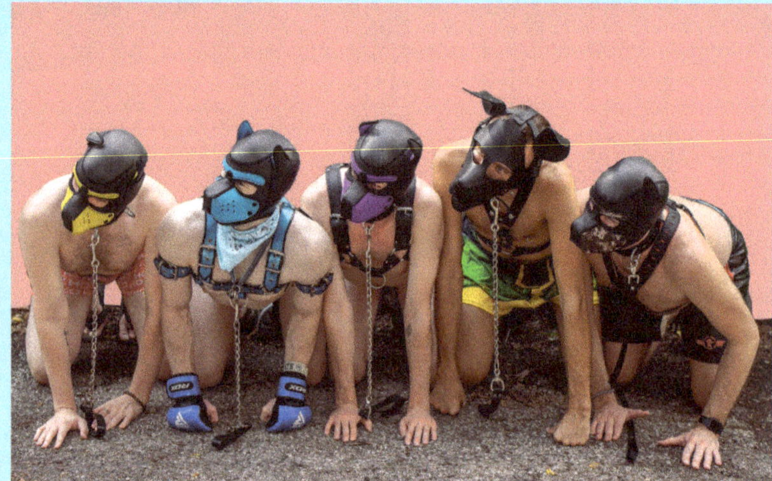

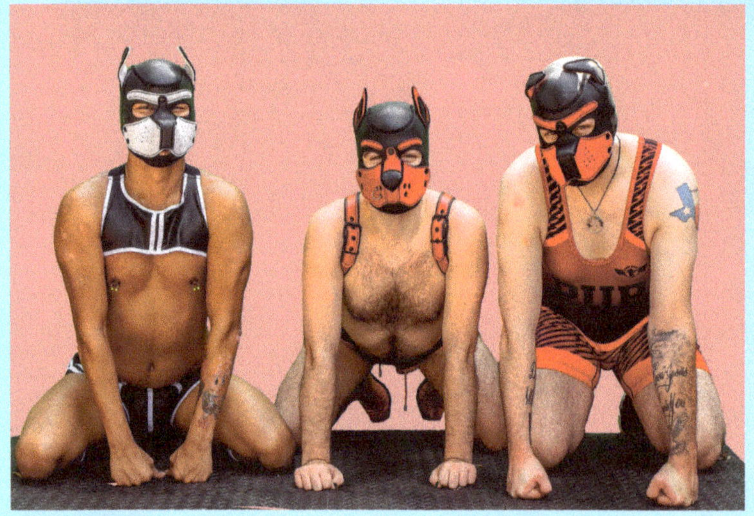

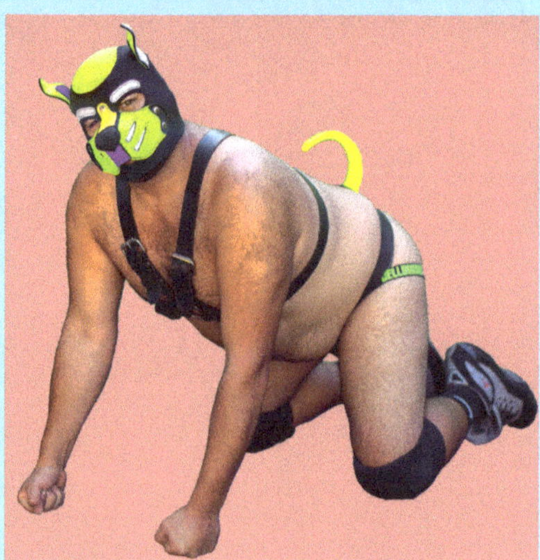

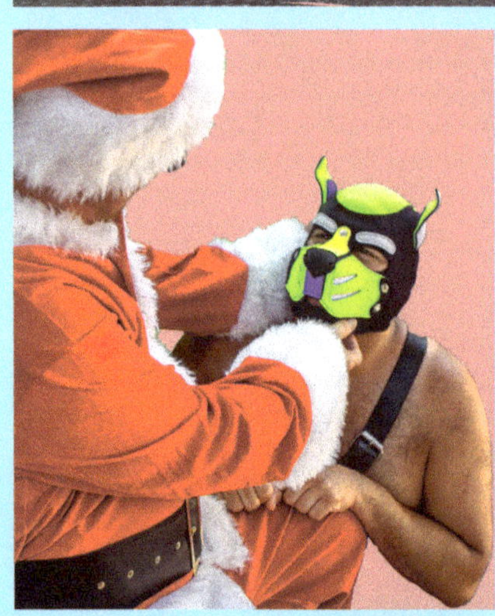

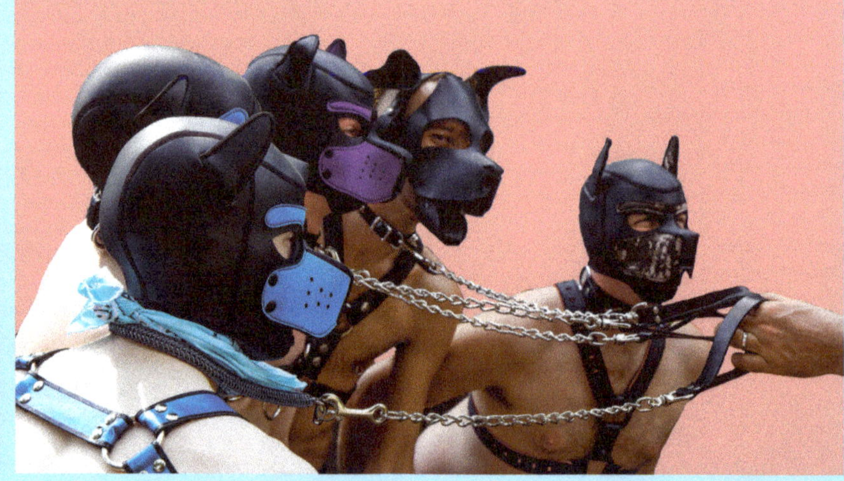

he loves every pup?

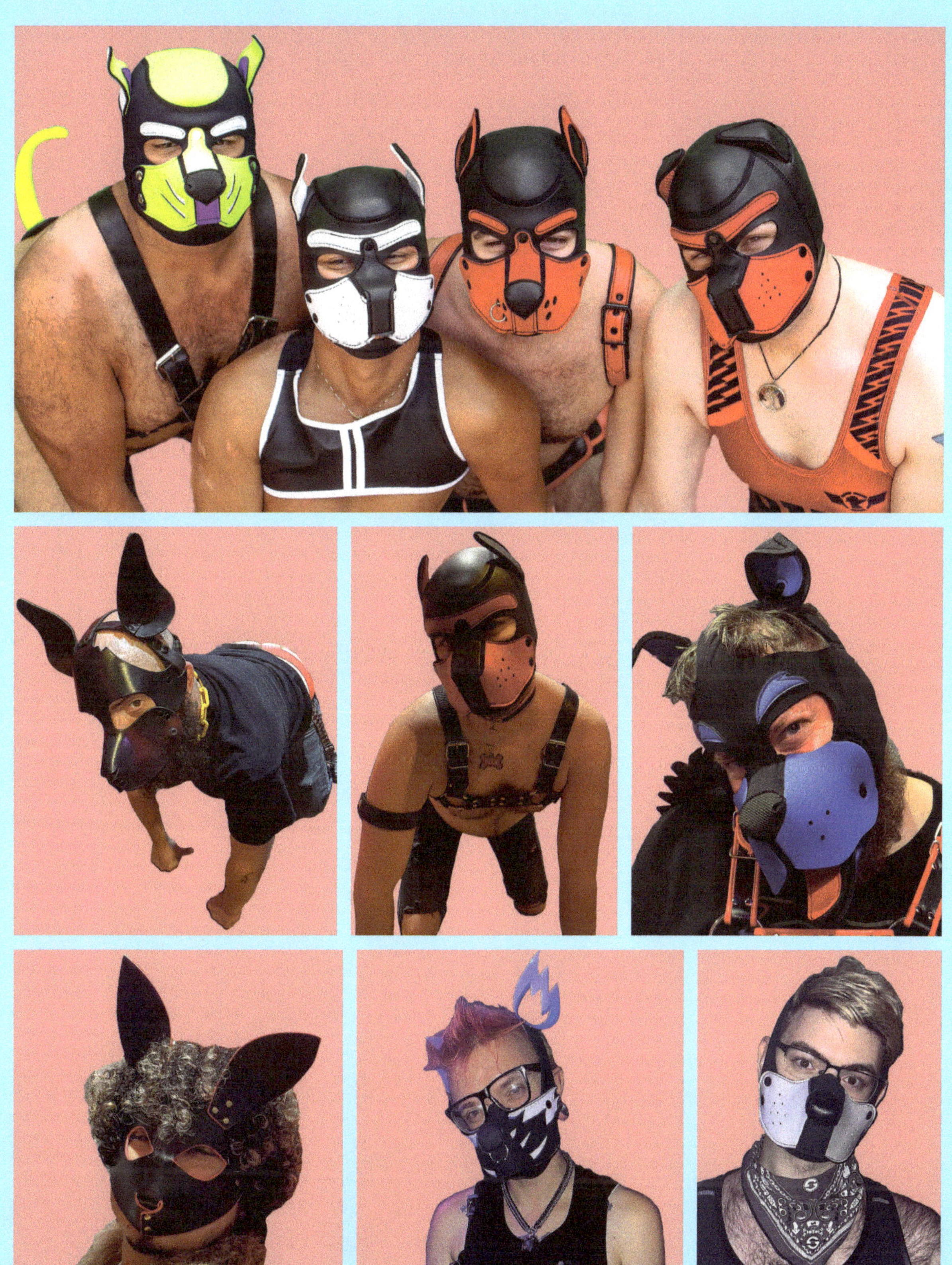

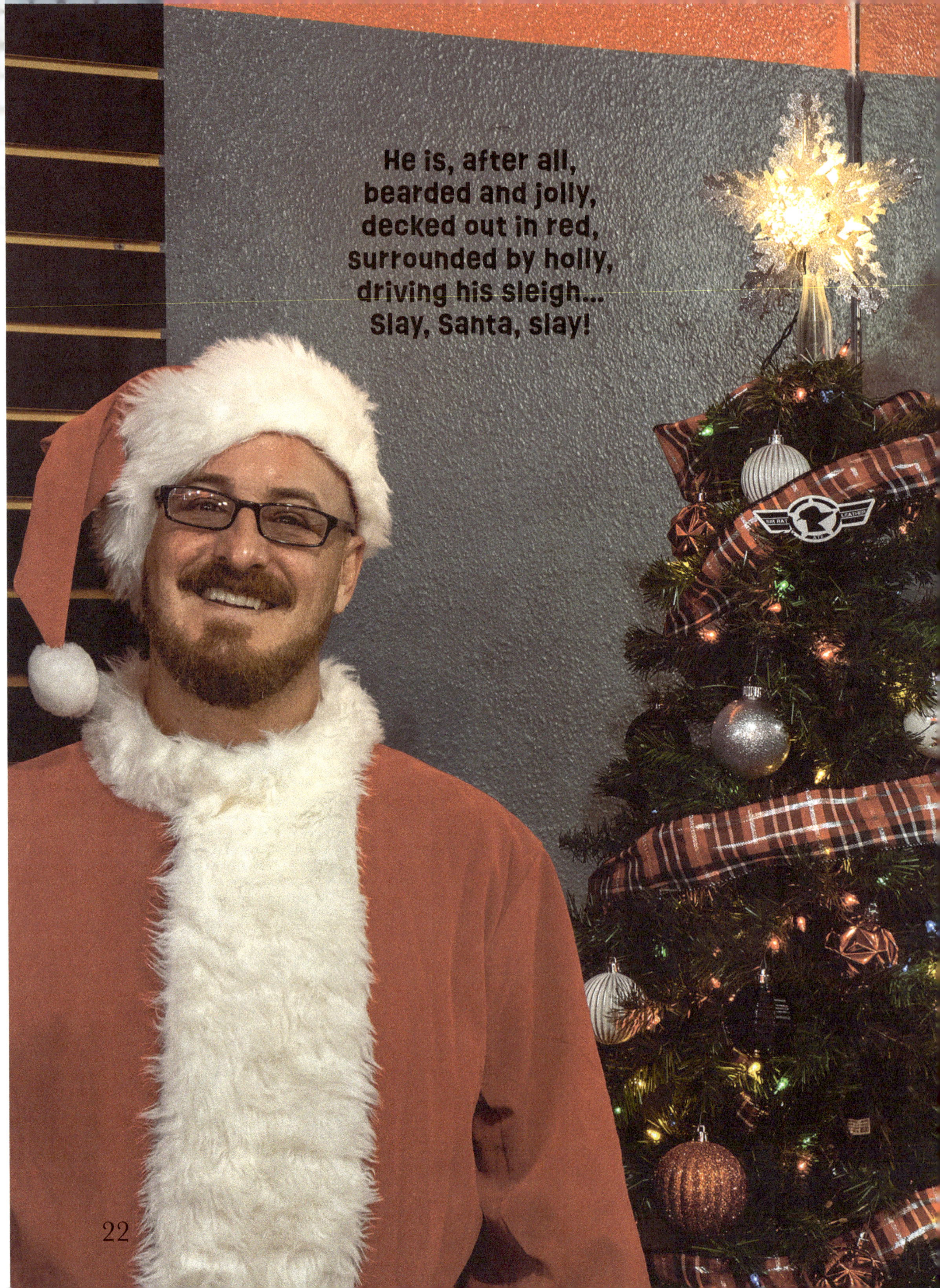

He is, after all,
bearded and jolly,
decked out in red,
surrounded by holly,
driving his sleigh...
Slay, Santa, slay!

His leather and fleece are fashionable fare.
What if Santa's a Bear?
(You know the kind.)

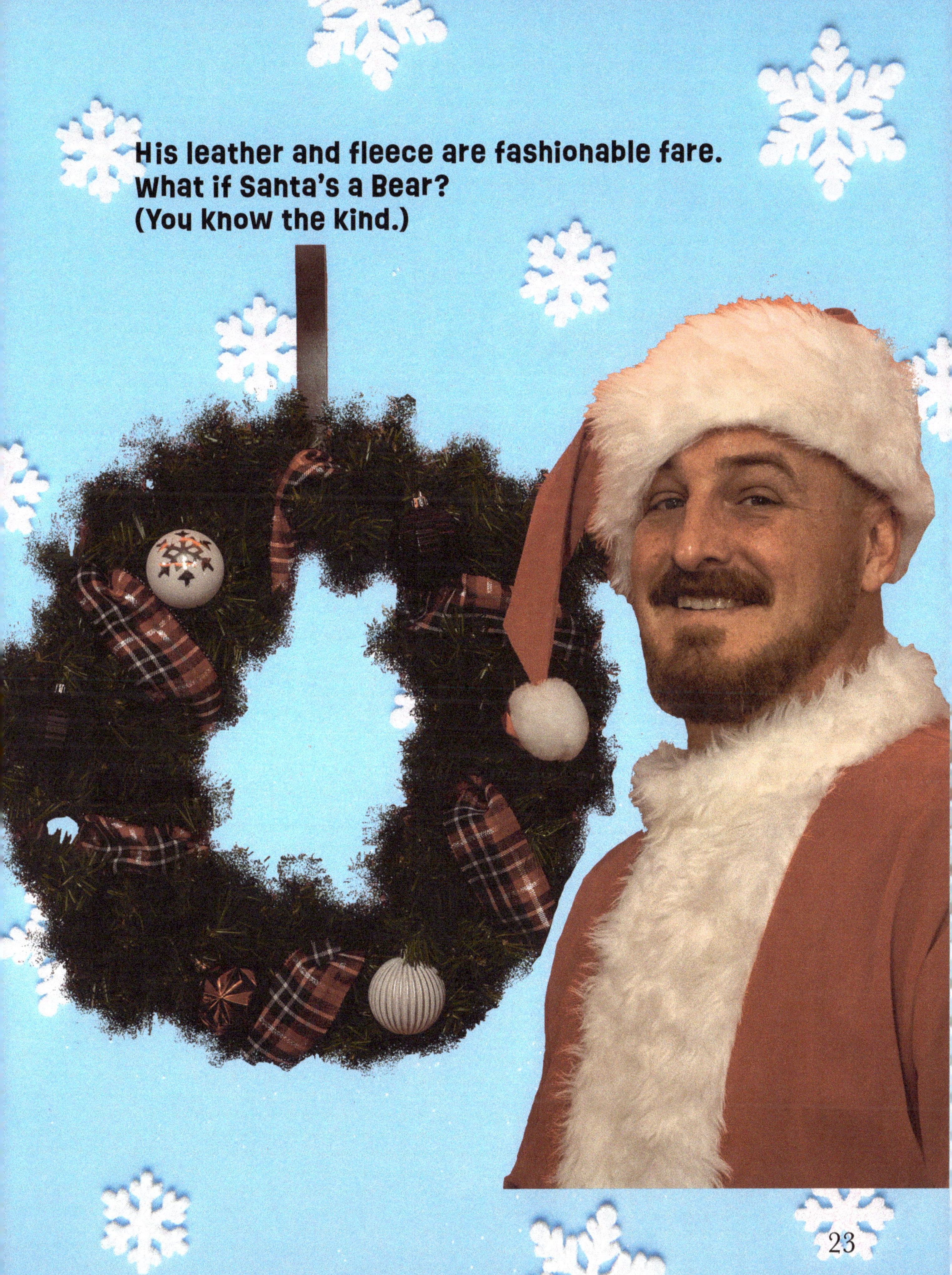

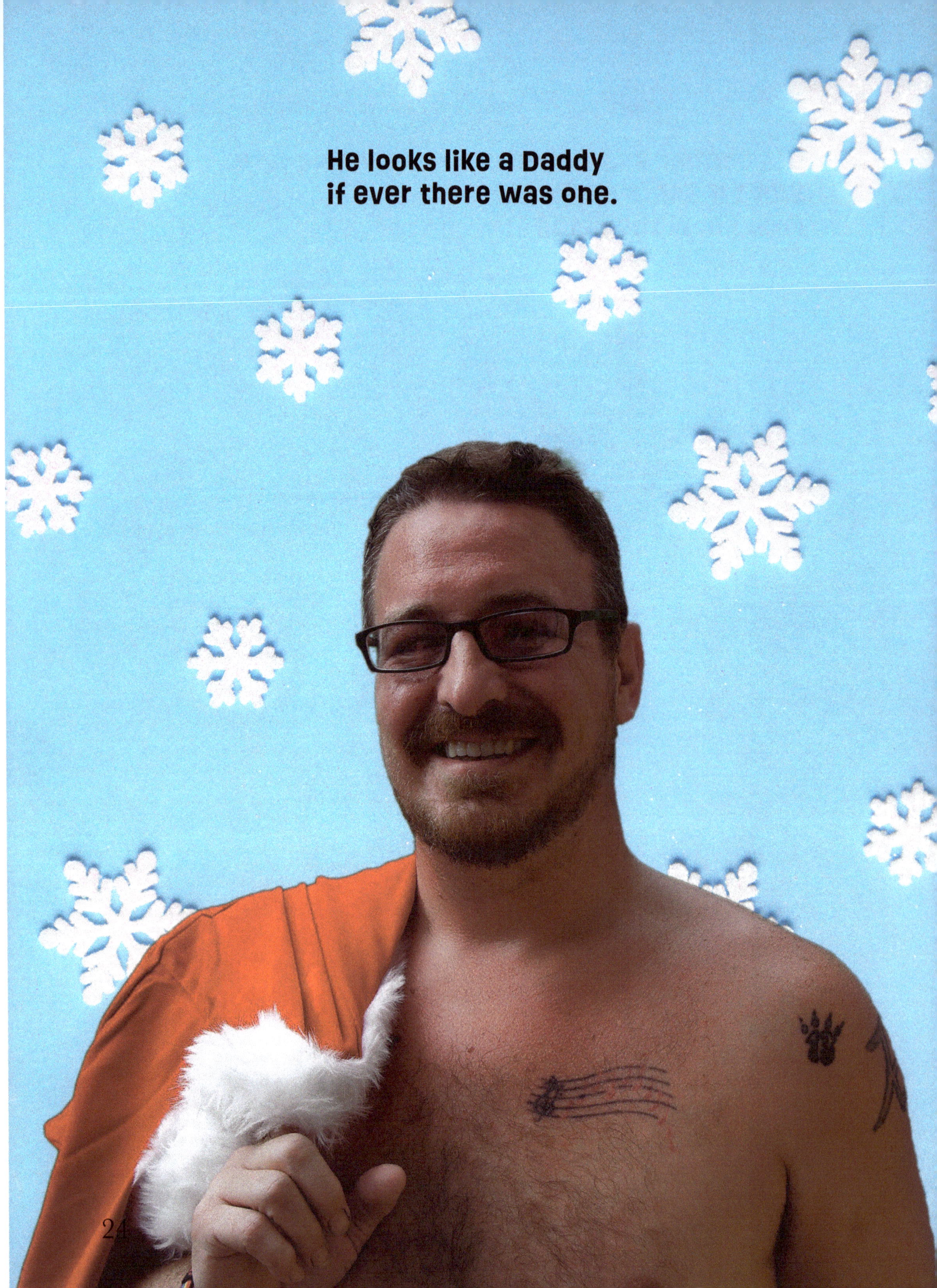
He looks like a Daddy
if ever there was one.

Climb up on his knee.
You'll see.

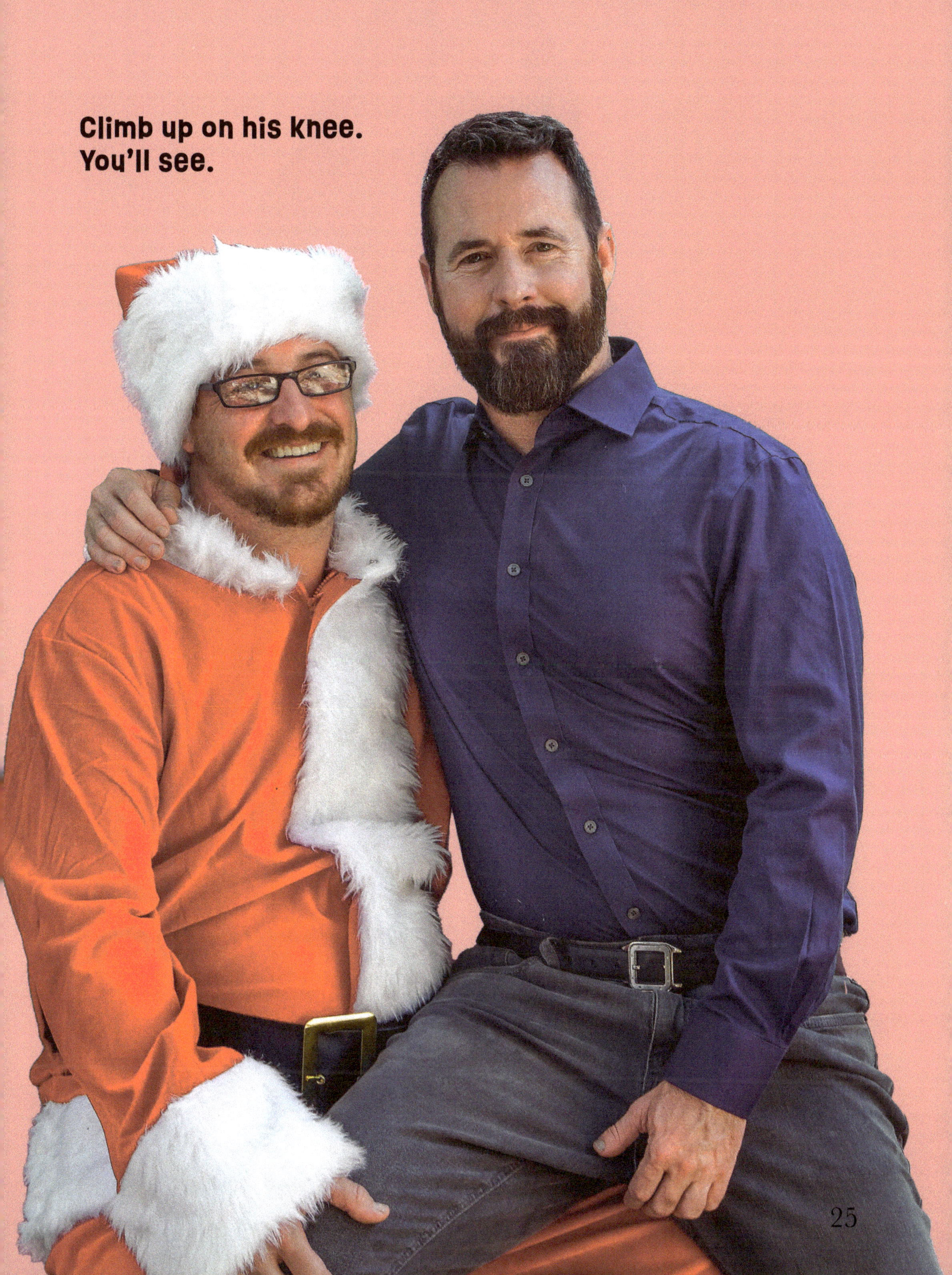

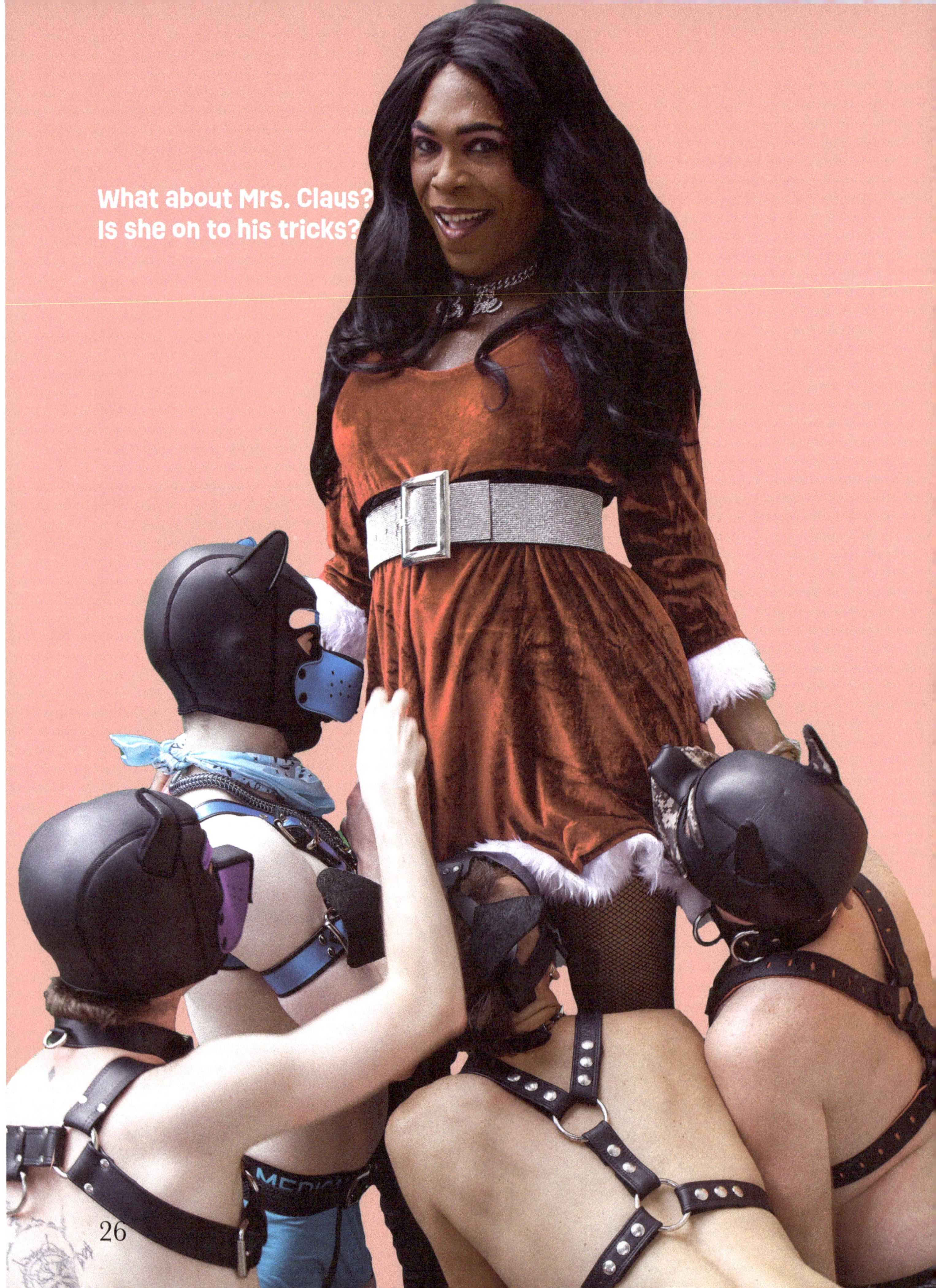

What about Mrs. Claus?
Is she on to his tricks?

They say she always gets her way
and only good boys pull her sleigh
(very good boys).

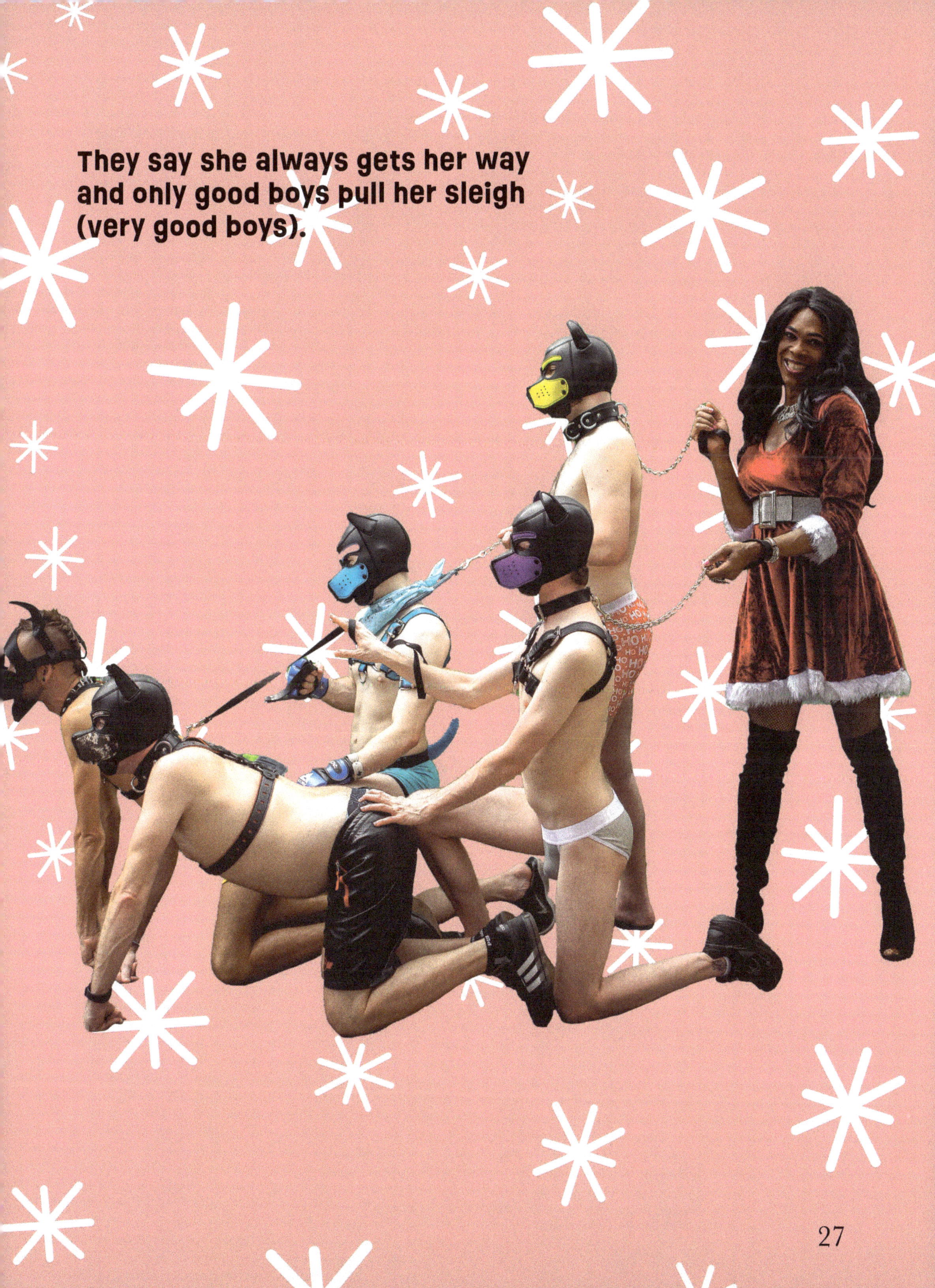

Wait a minute!
Who is this?
Who are they?

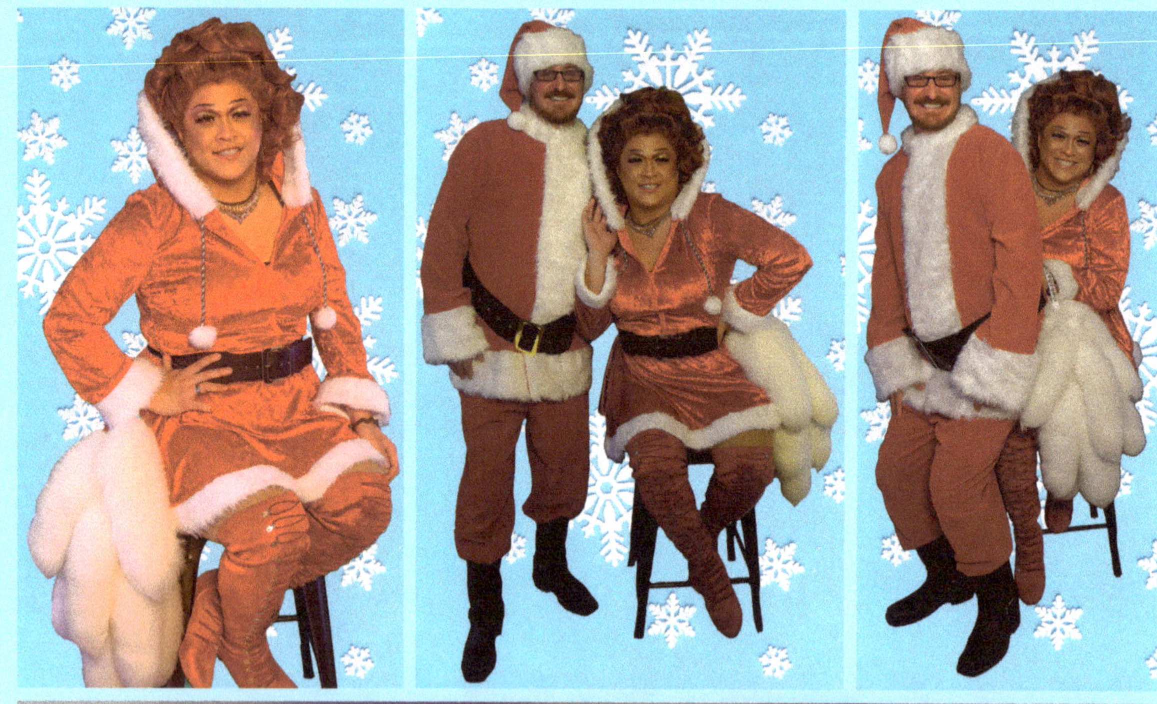

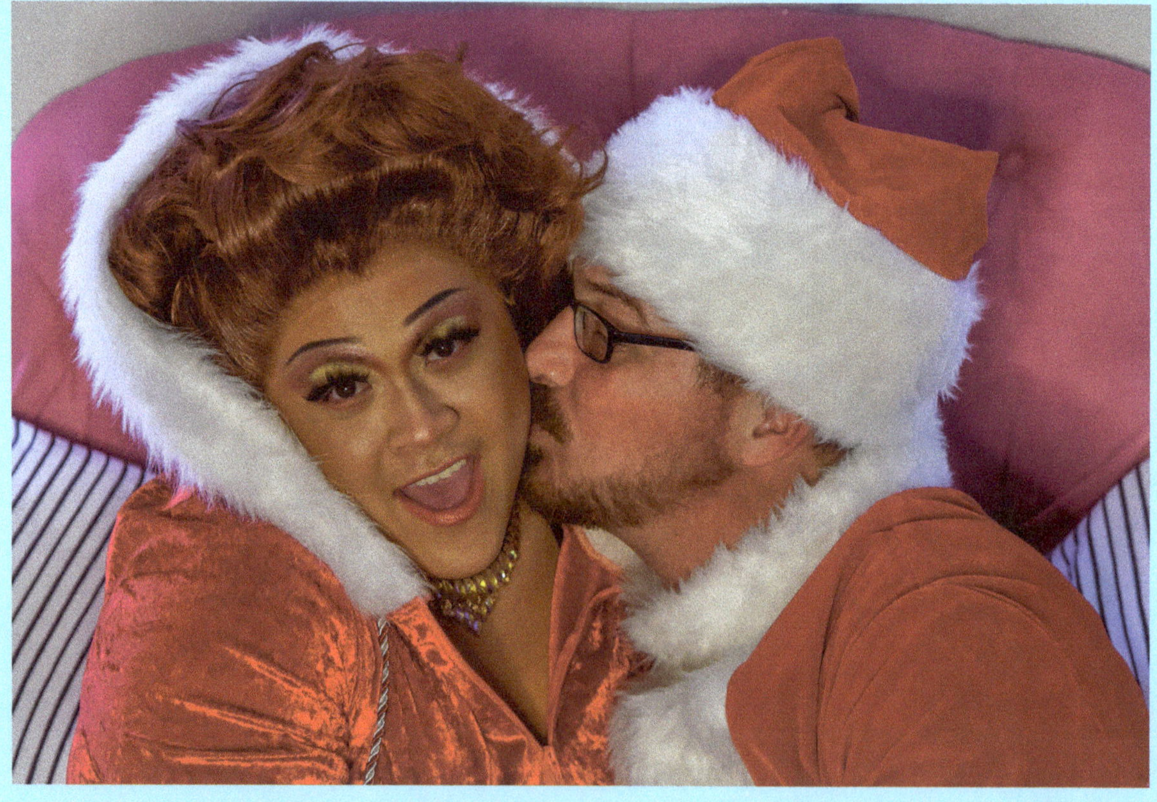

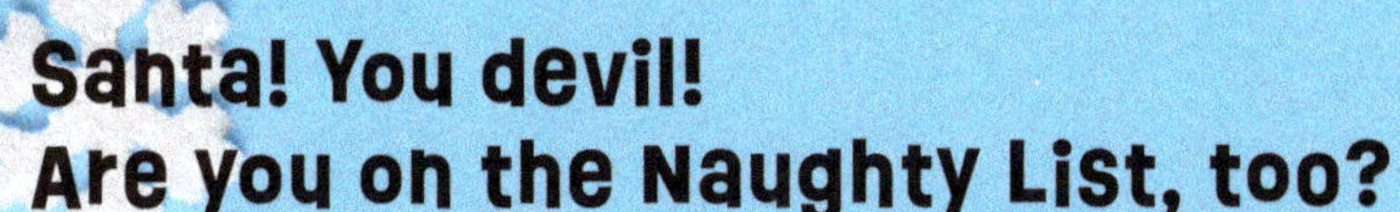

Santa! You devil!
Are you on the Naughty List, too?

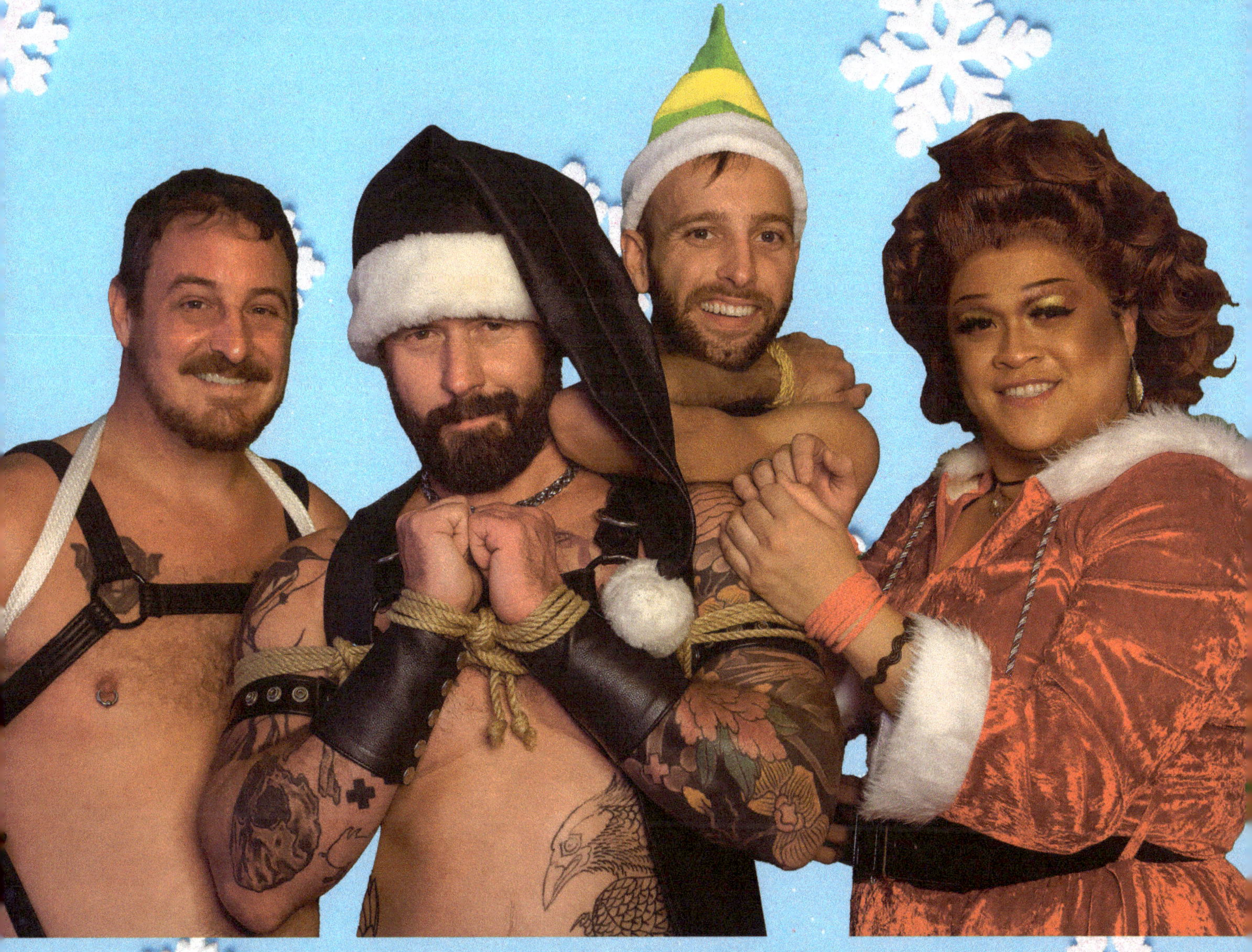

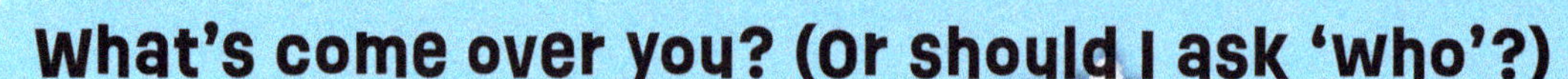
What's come over you? (Or should I ask 'who'?)

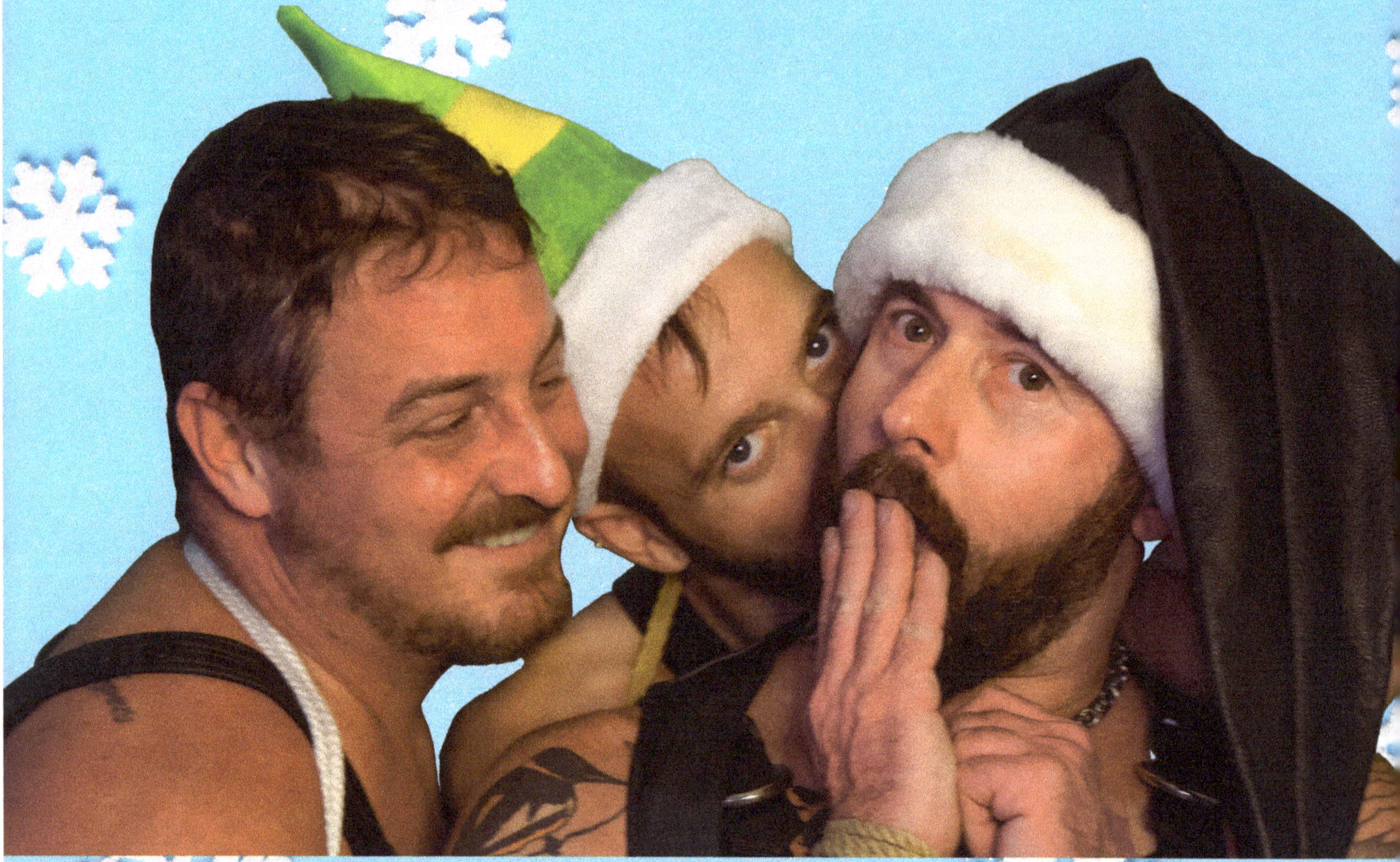

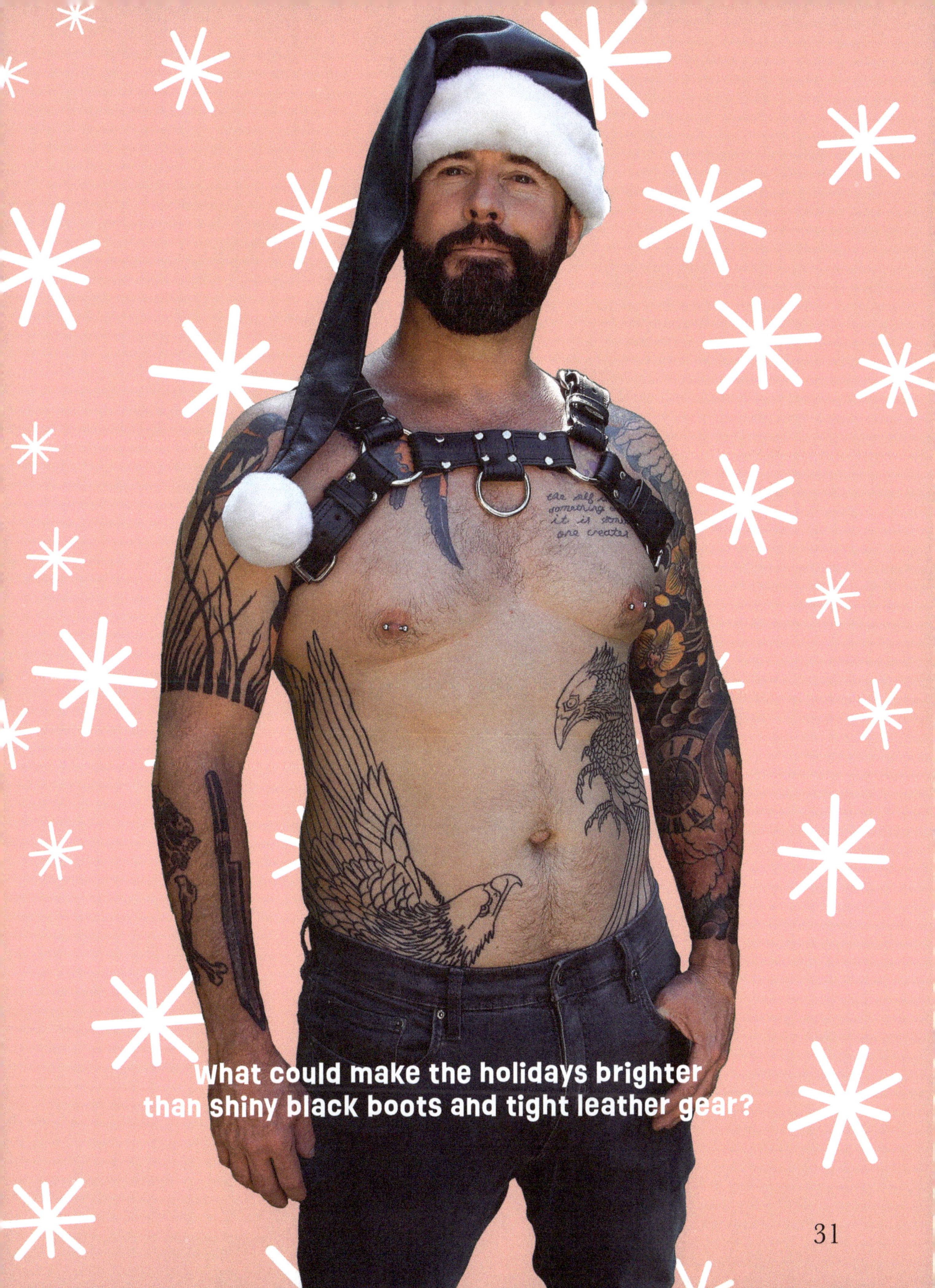

What could make the holidays brighter
than shiny black boots and tight leather gear?

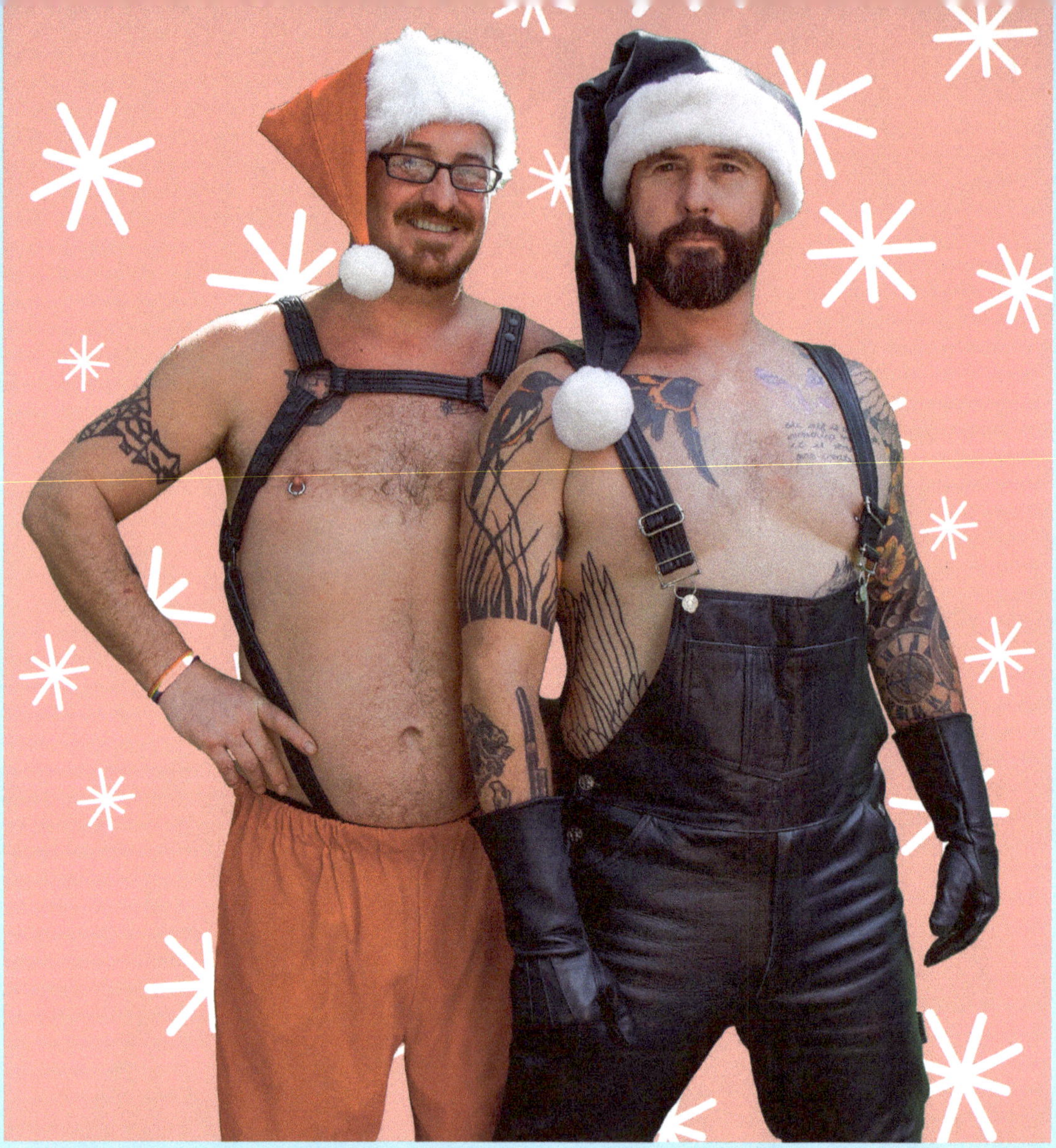

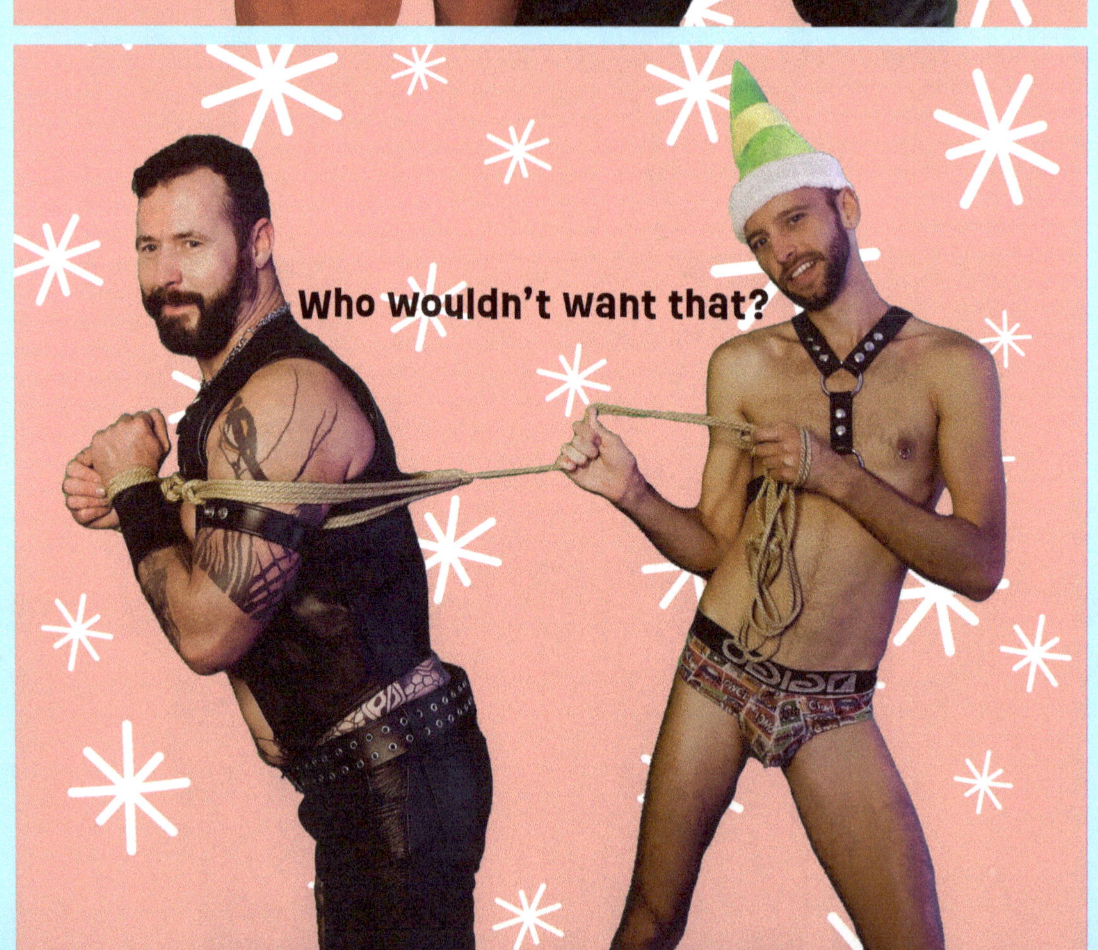
Who wouldn’t want that?

What's there to fear?

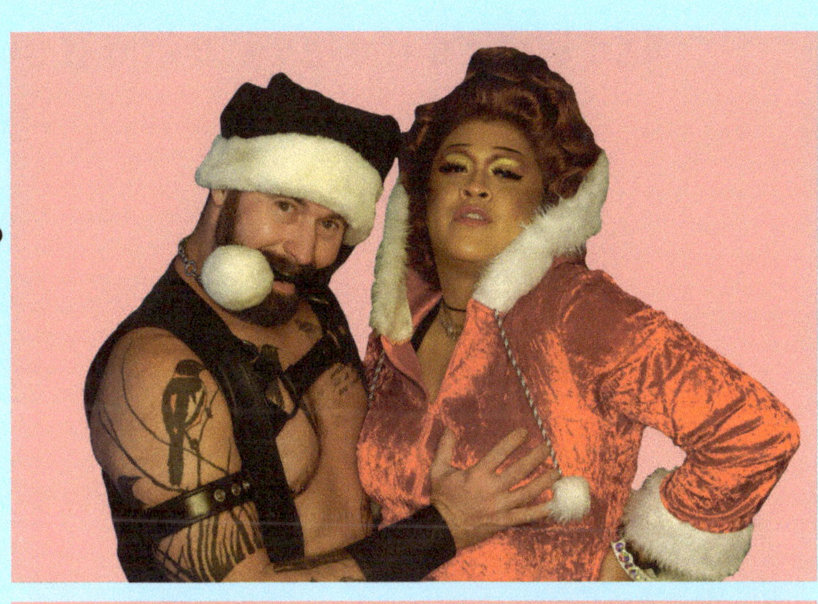

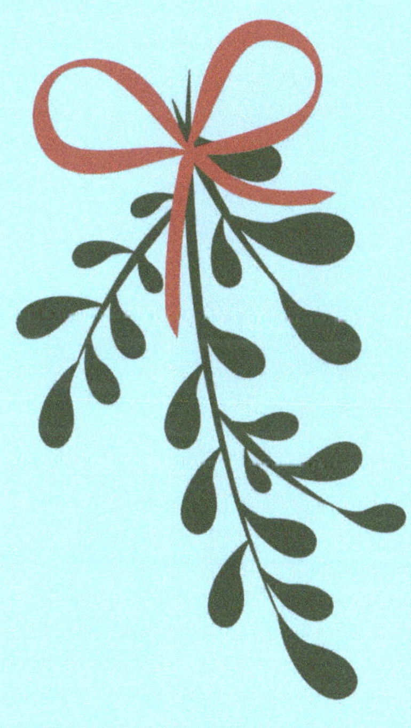

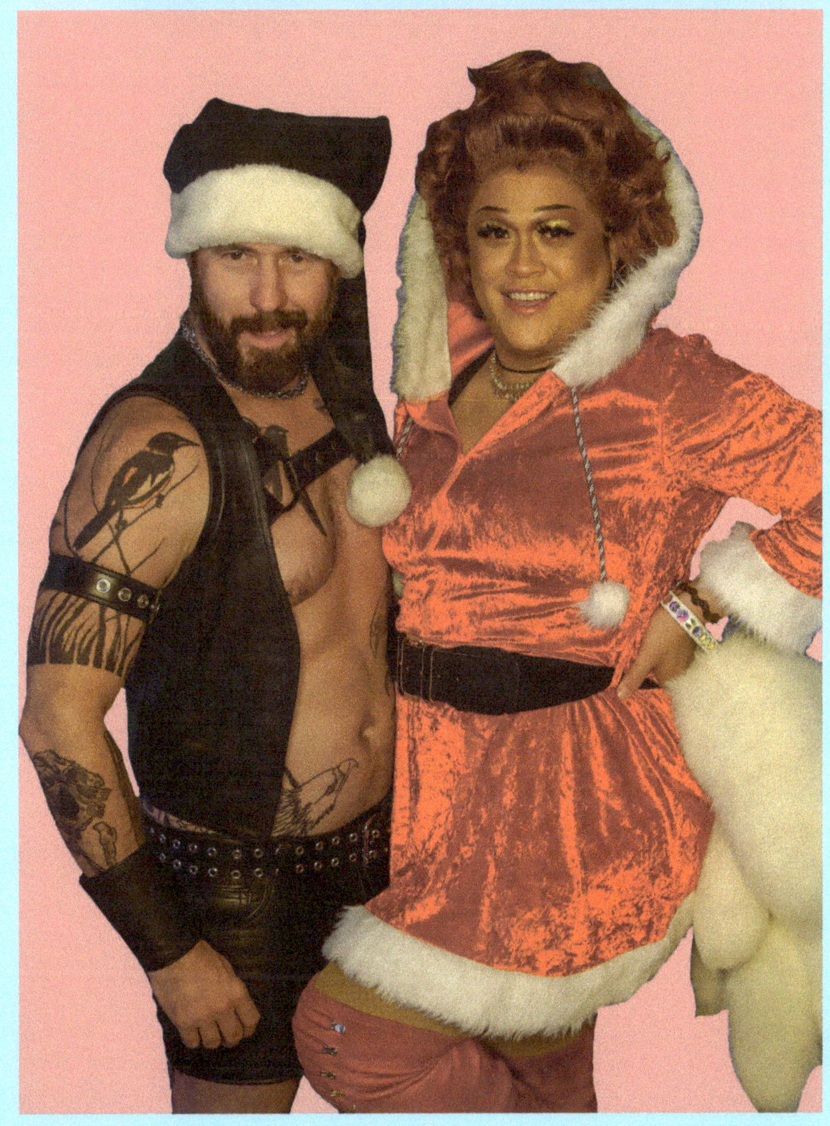

And what's there to dread if snuggled in bed

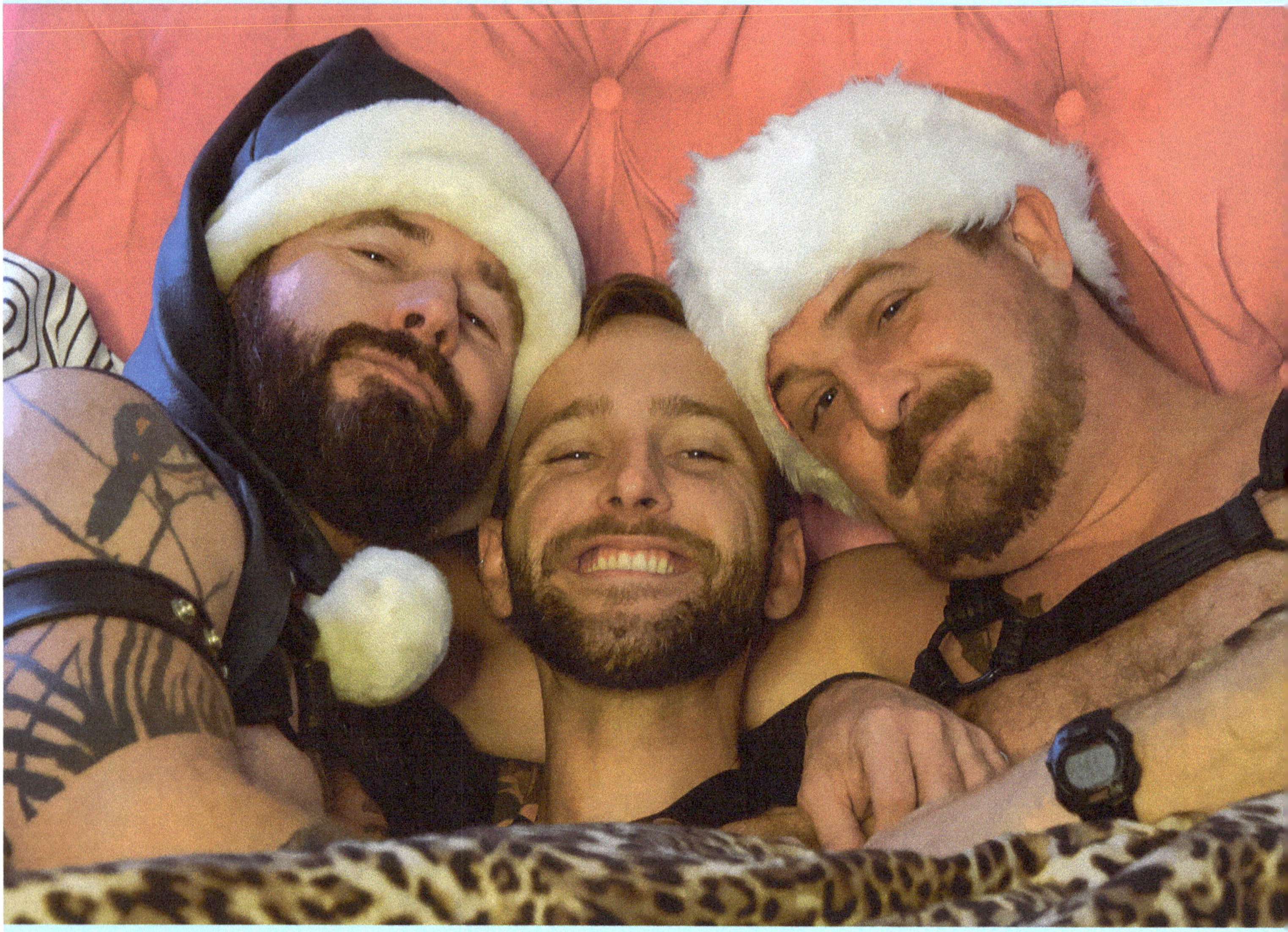

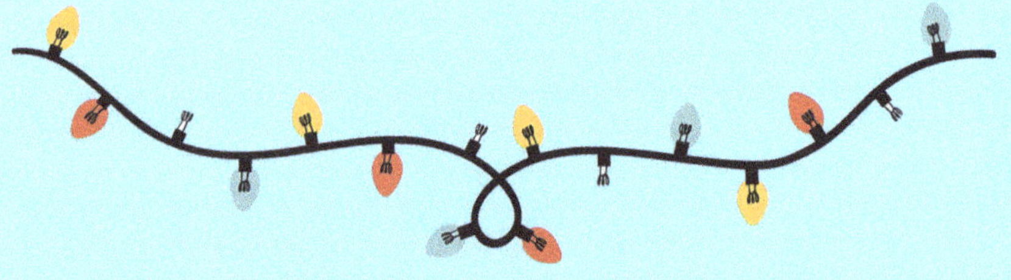

are sugarplum fairies getting some gingerbread?

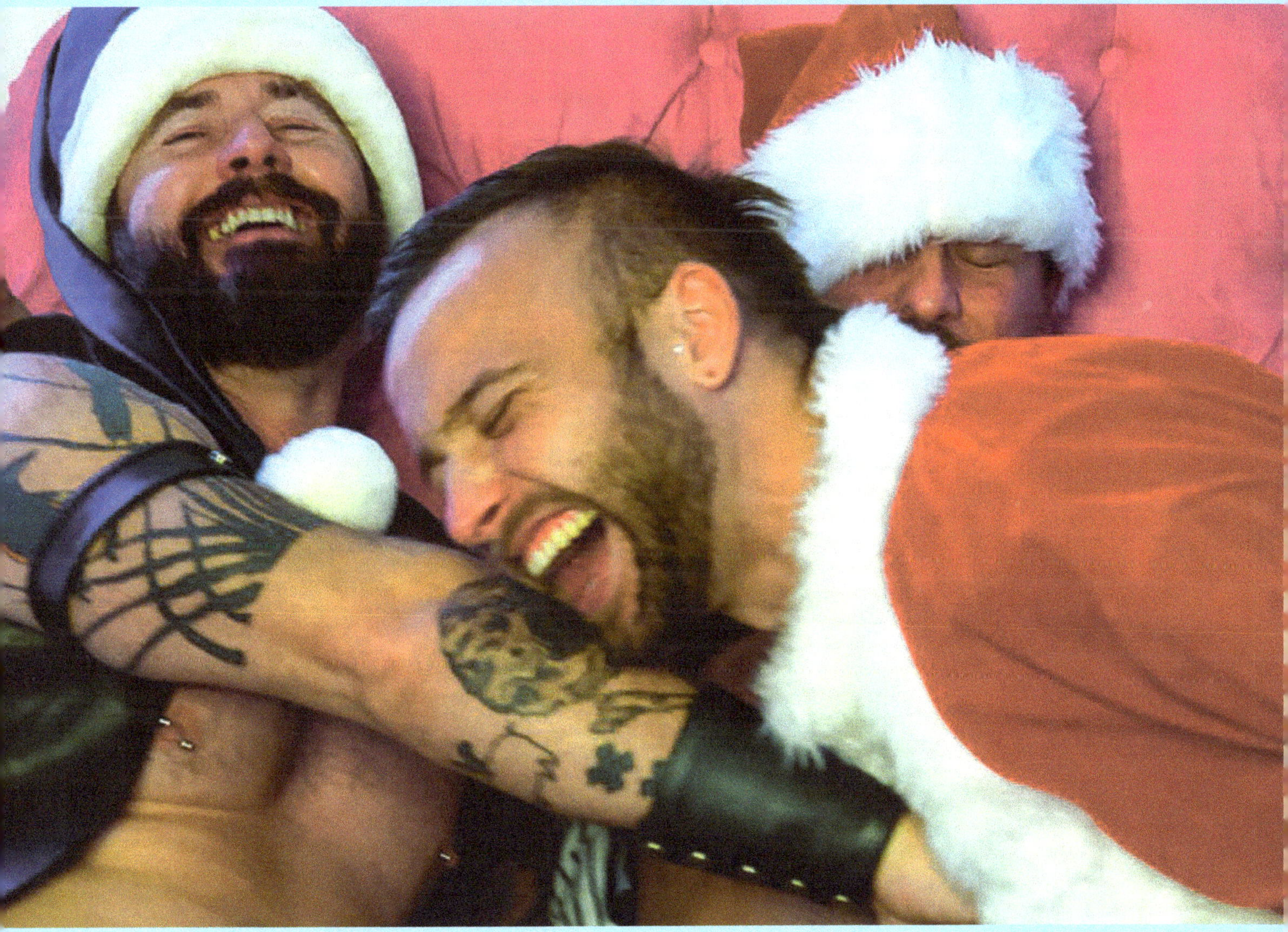

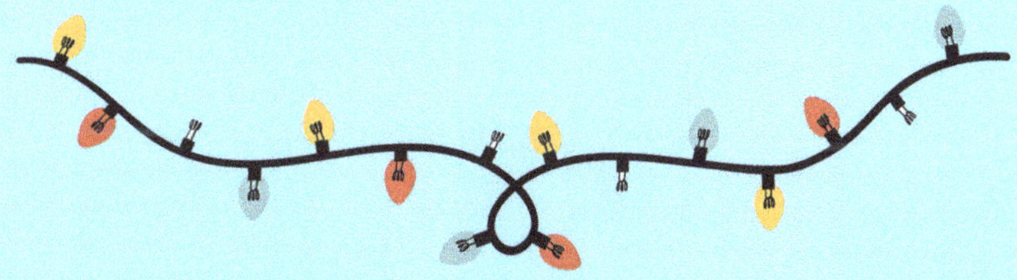

Gingerbread rhymes with bed. What were you thinking?

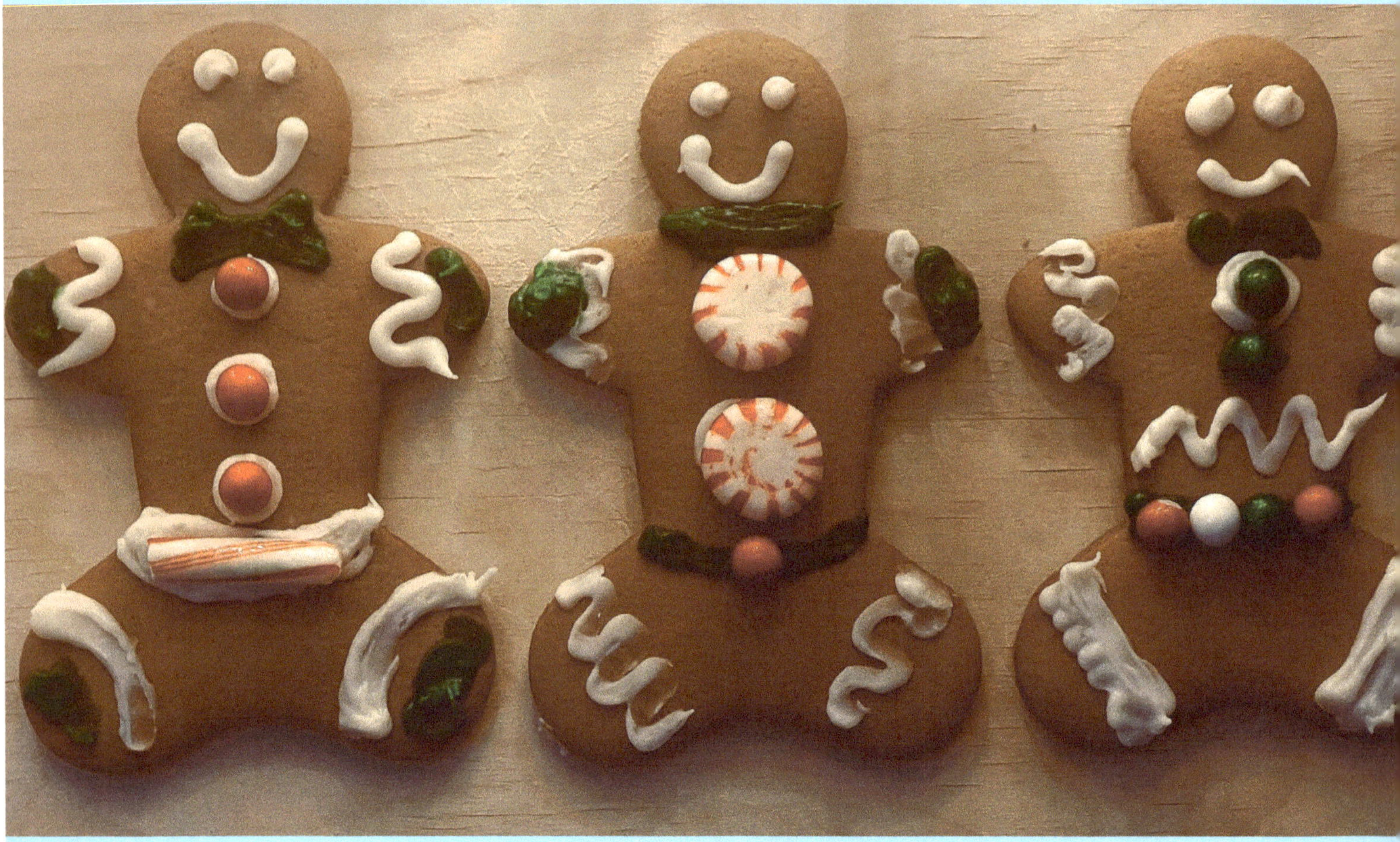

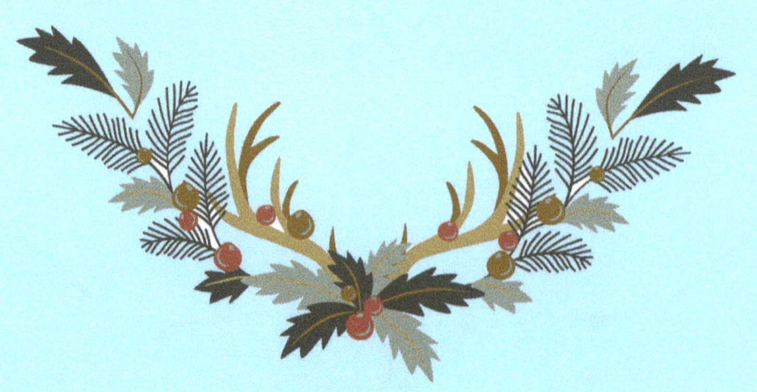

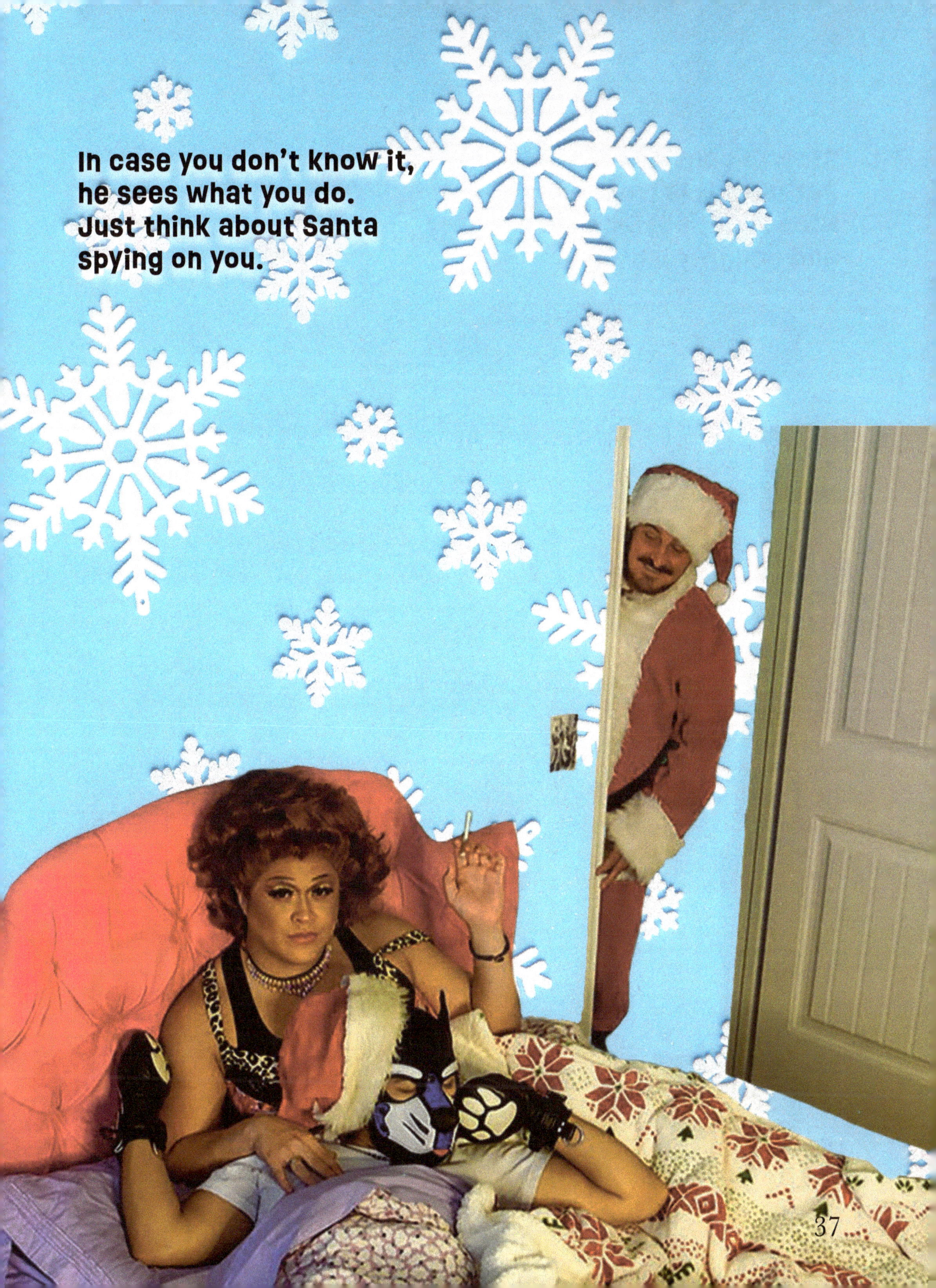
In case you don't know it,
he sees what you do.
Just think about Santa
spying on you.

Stop to consider.
Perhaps, it is true.
Nice is not better than naughty
and naughty isn't bad.

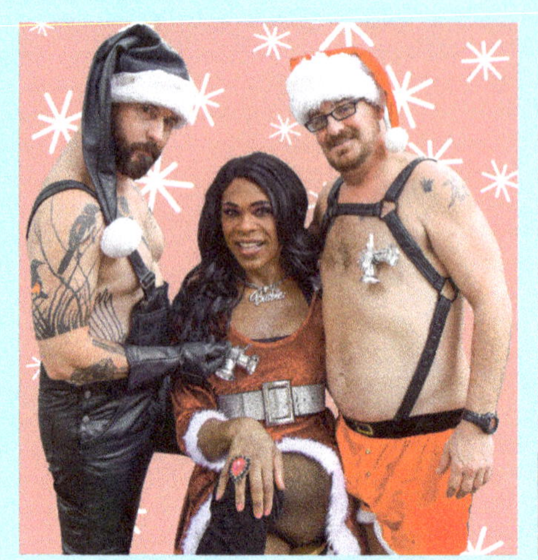

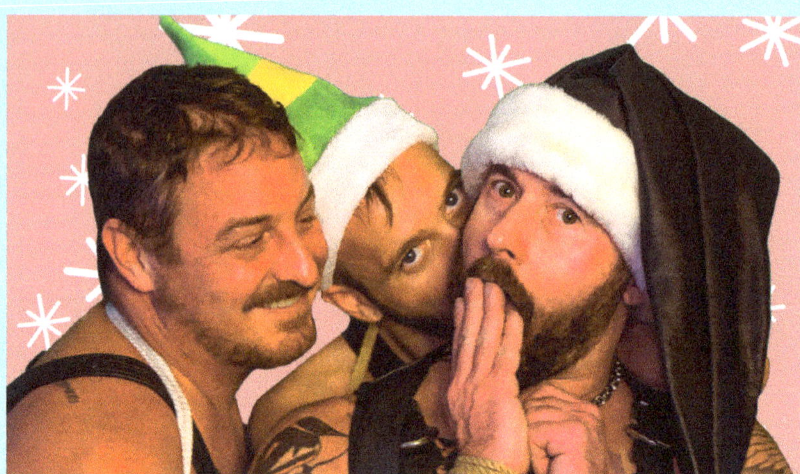

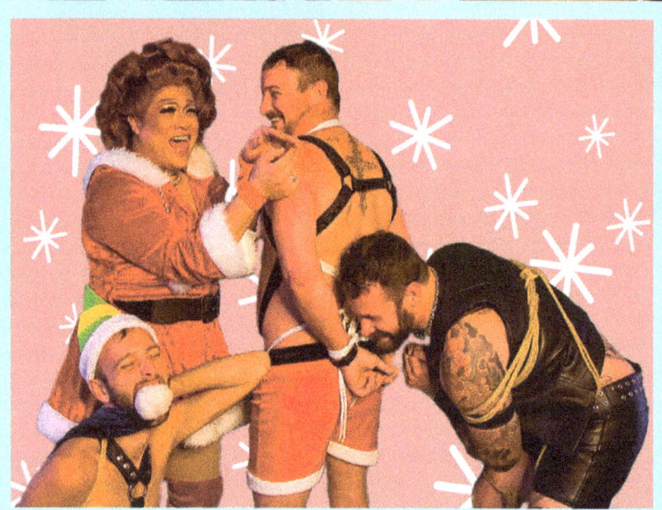

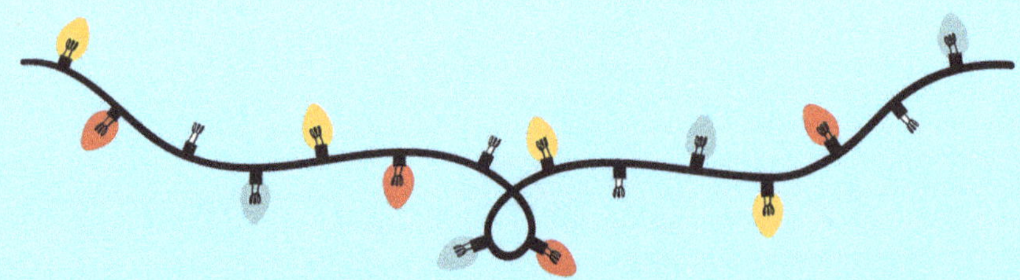

What if nice is just one way to make yourself glad?

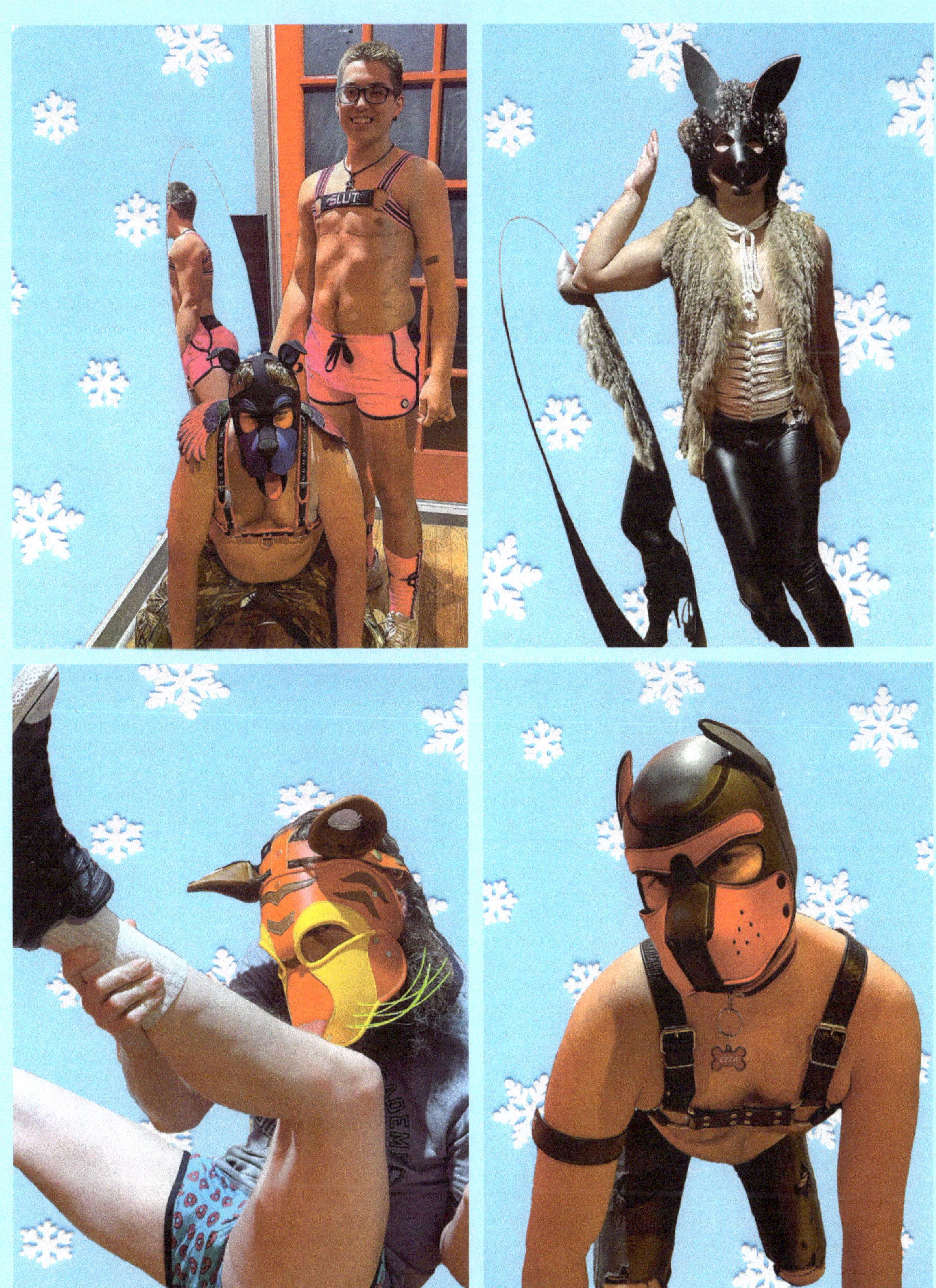

Santa's an equal opportunity elf who delivers a bounty to all who believe...

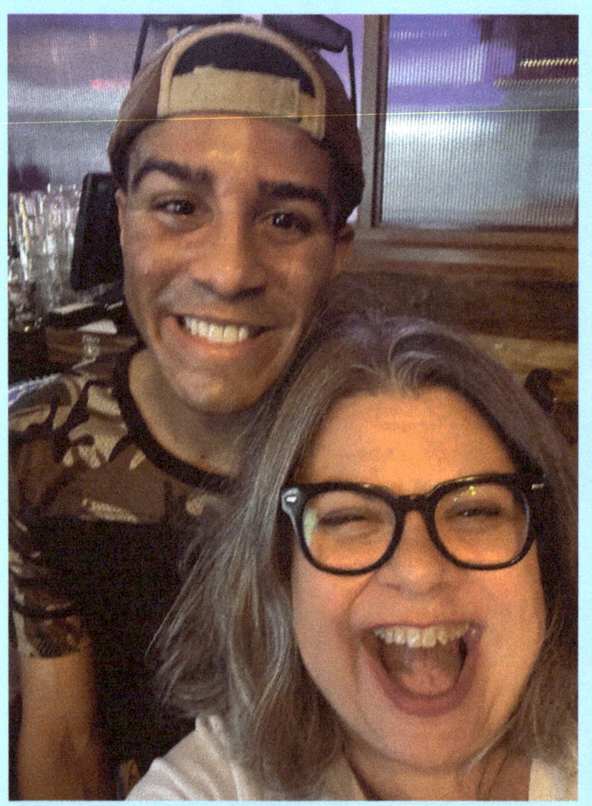

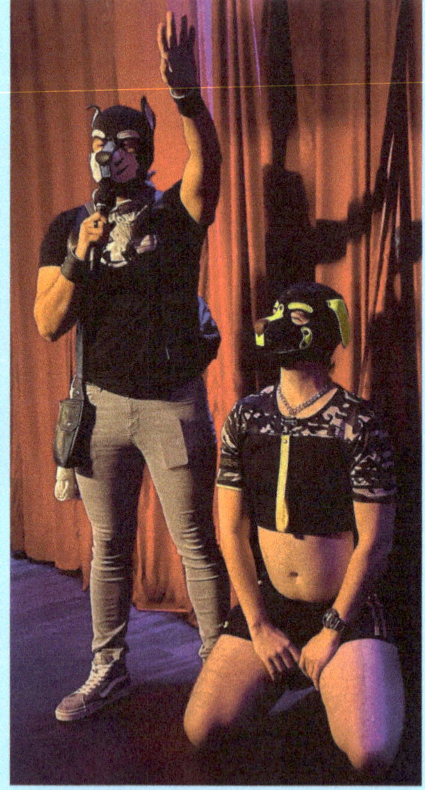

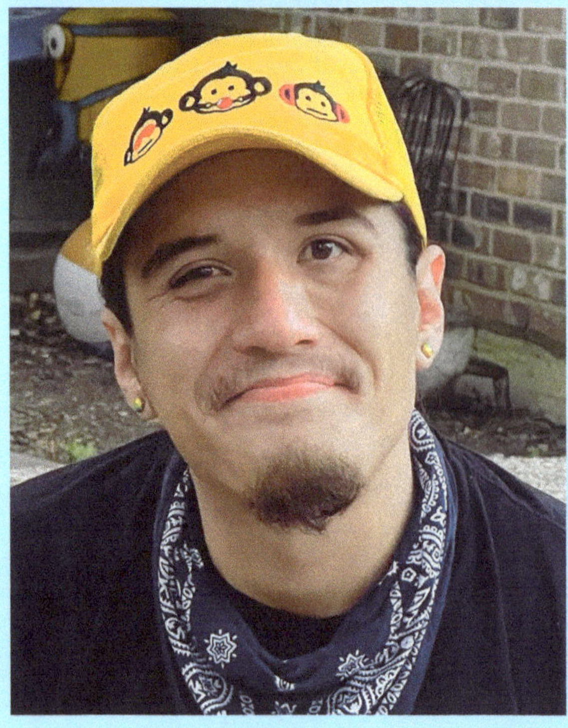

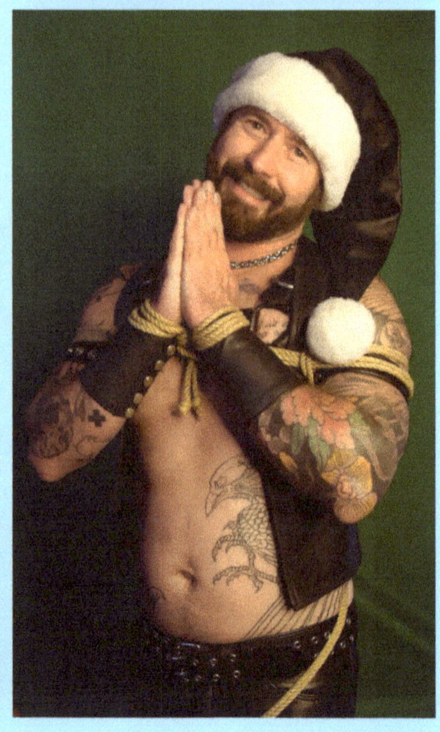

From the ho-ho-ho's to the go-go-go's

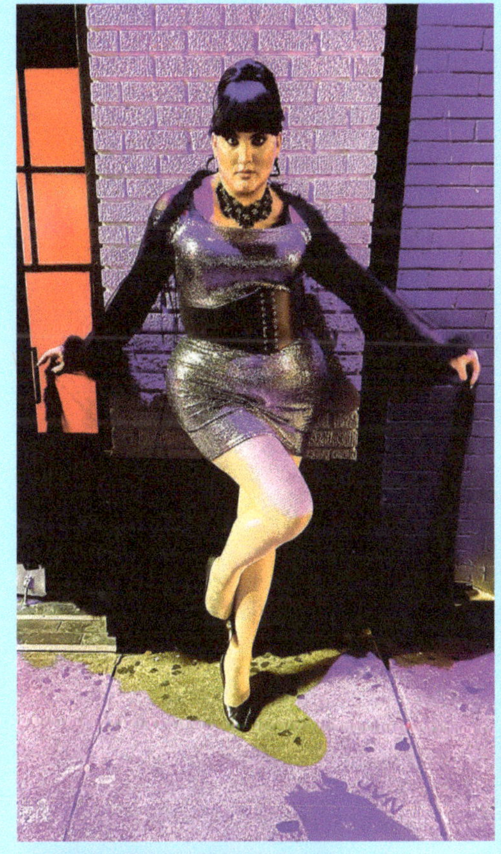

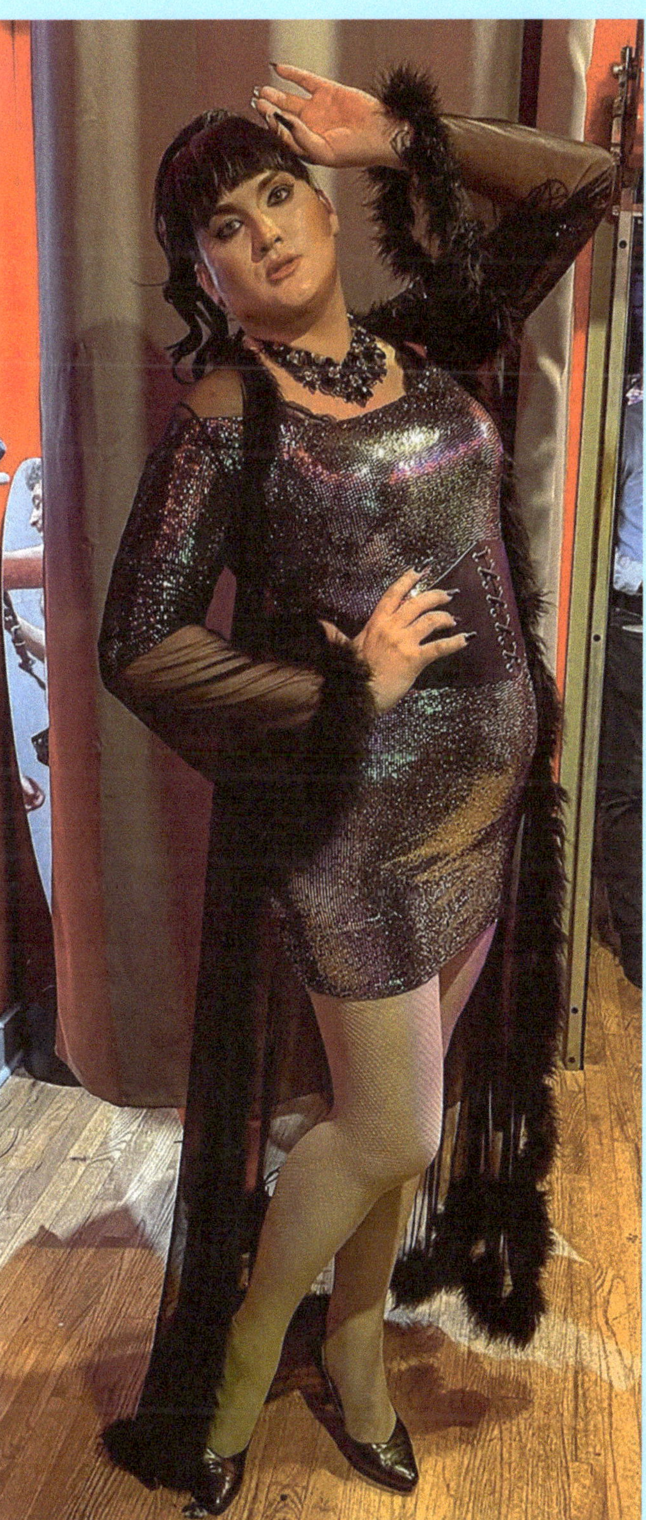

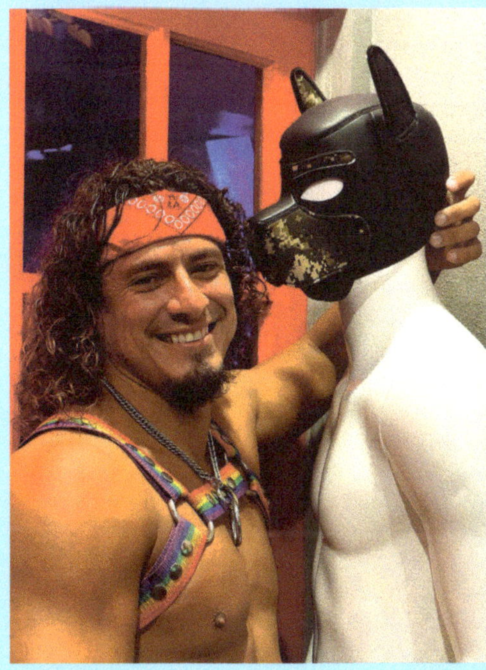

And to all who add XX to X-mas.

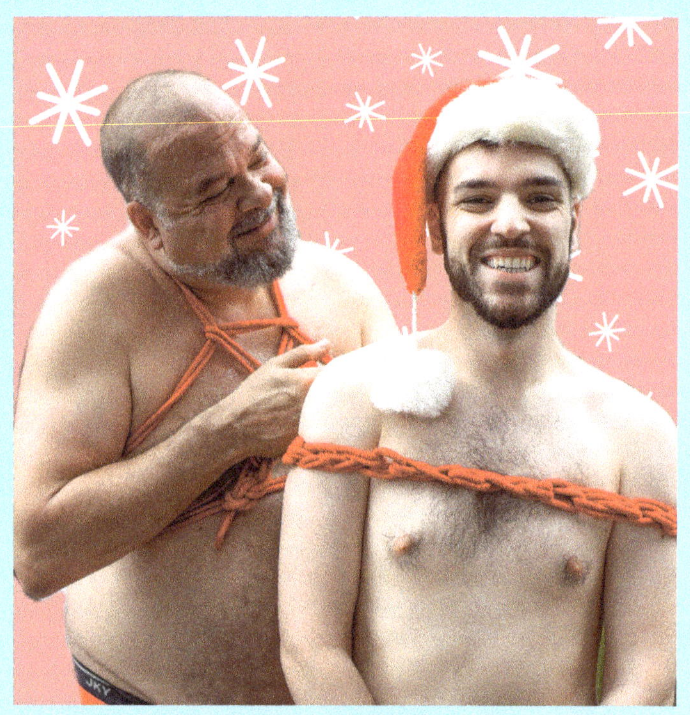

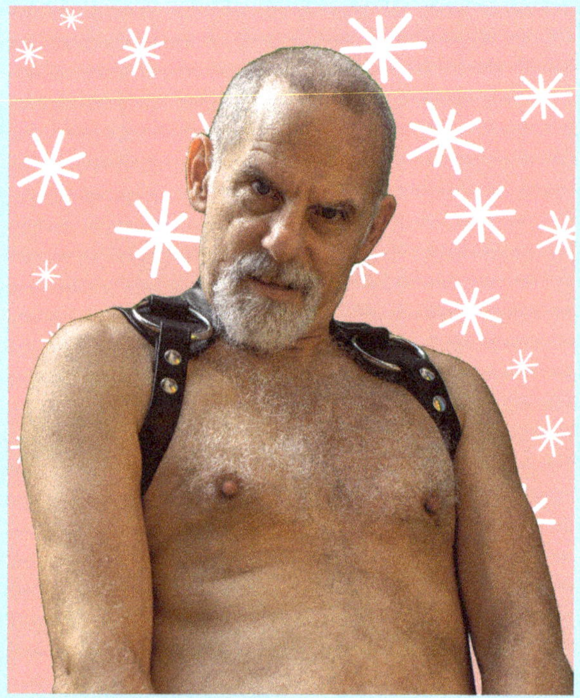

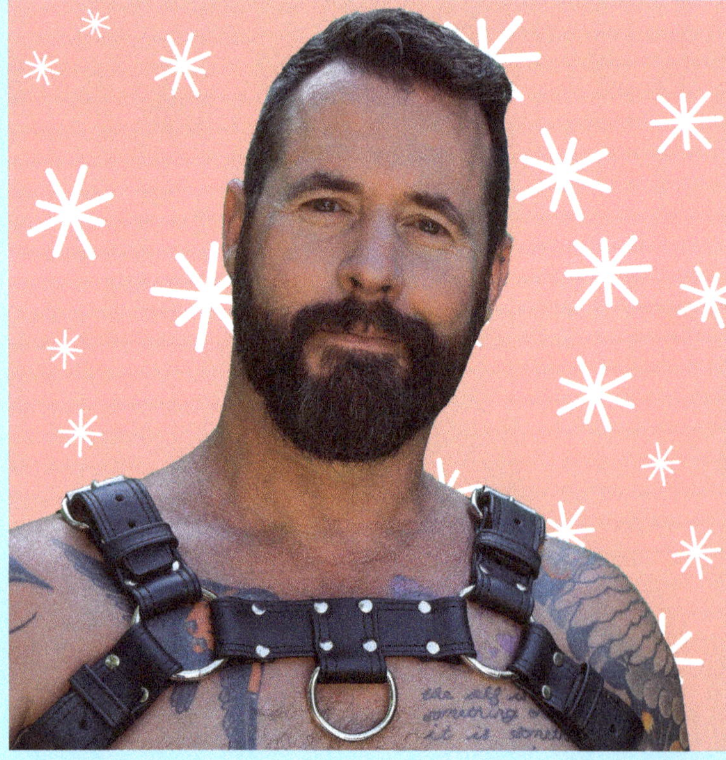

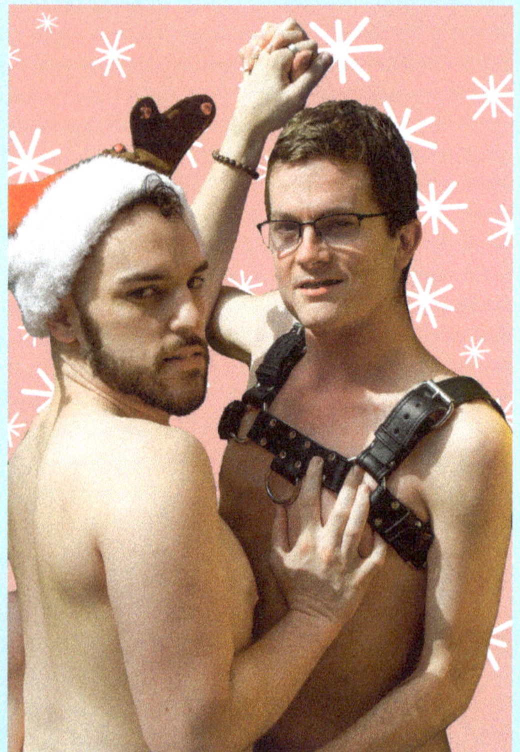

So, take heart, all you rascals!
Santa's coming all right.

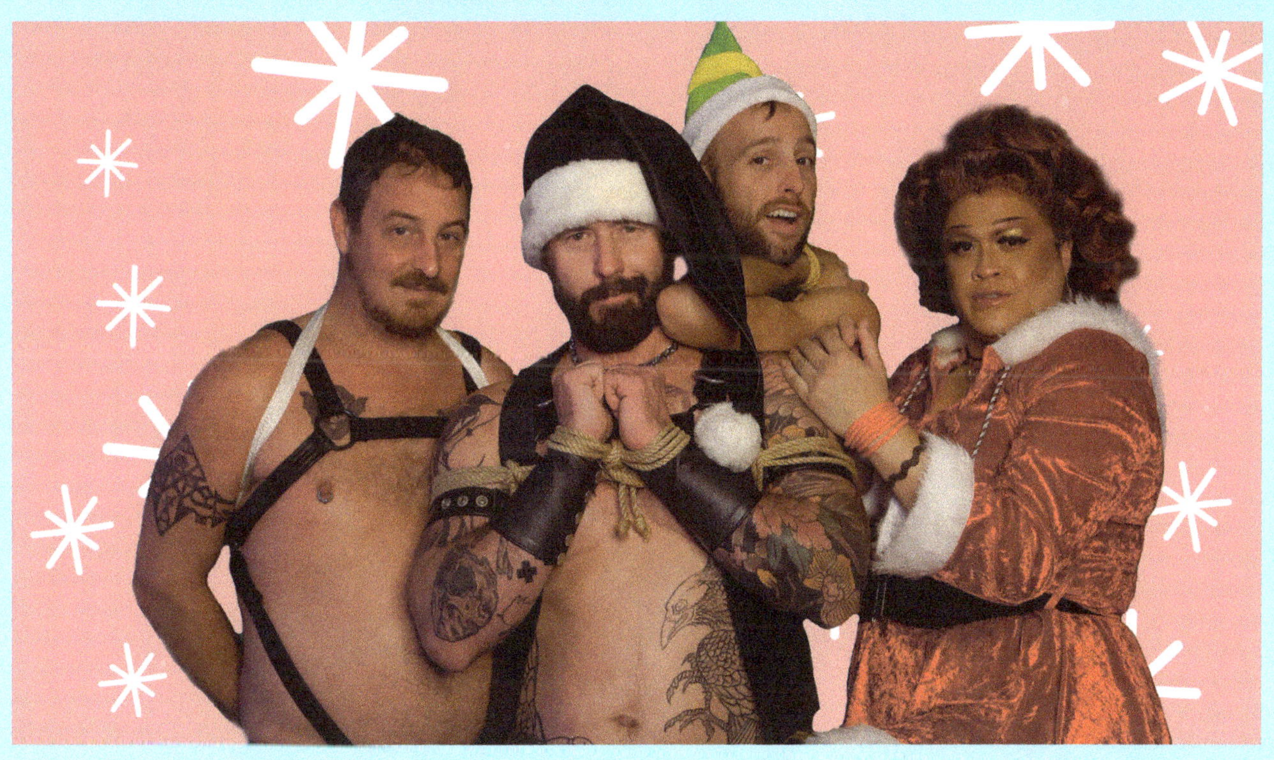

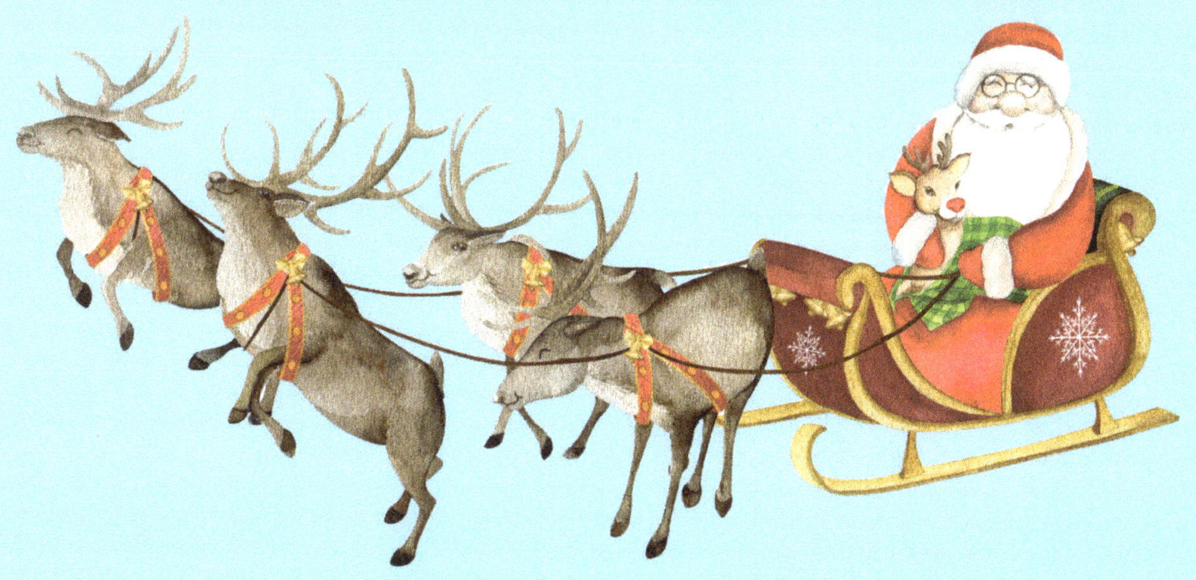

Merry XXX-mas to all

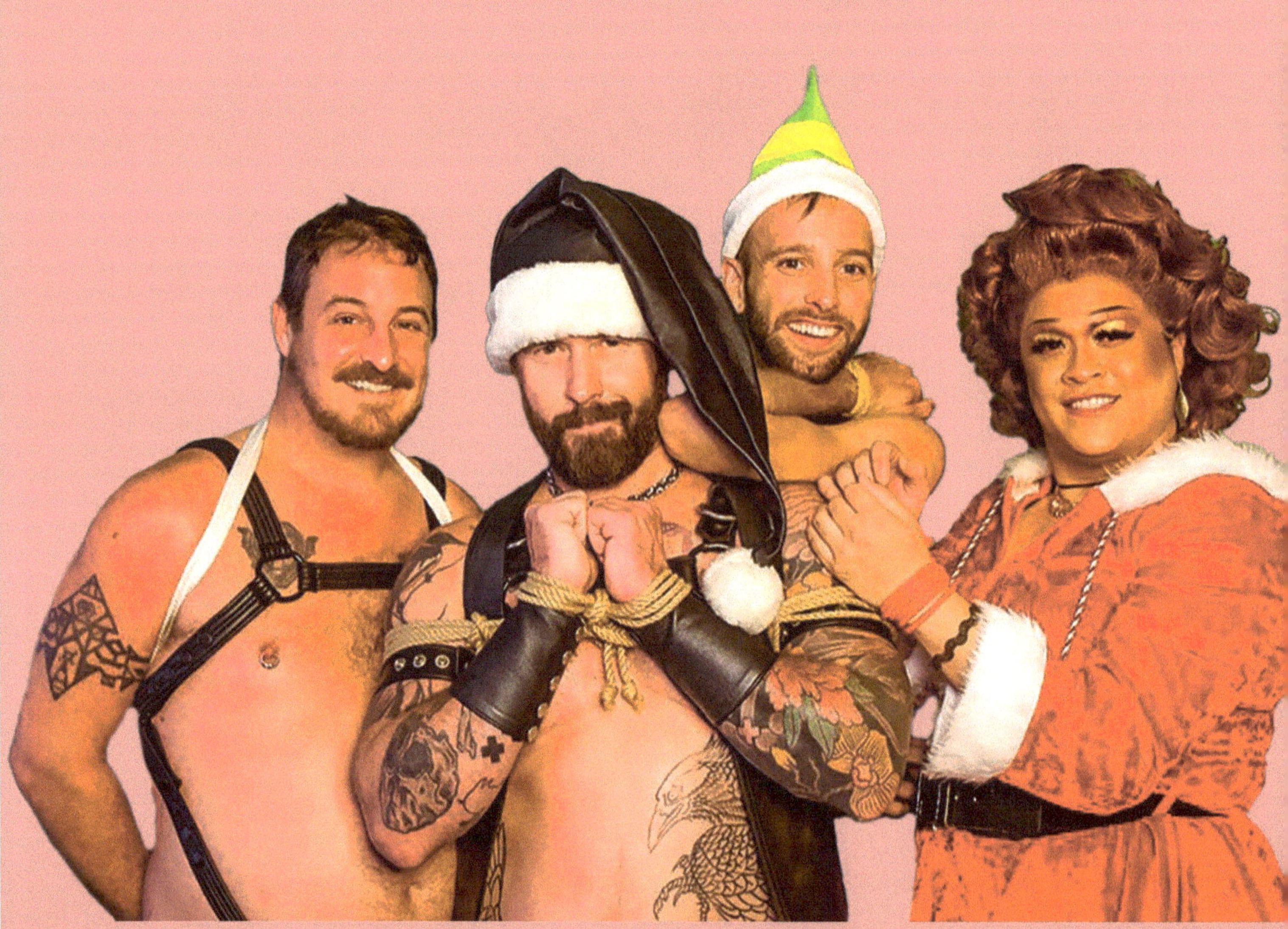

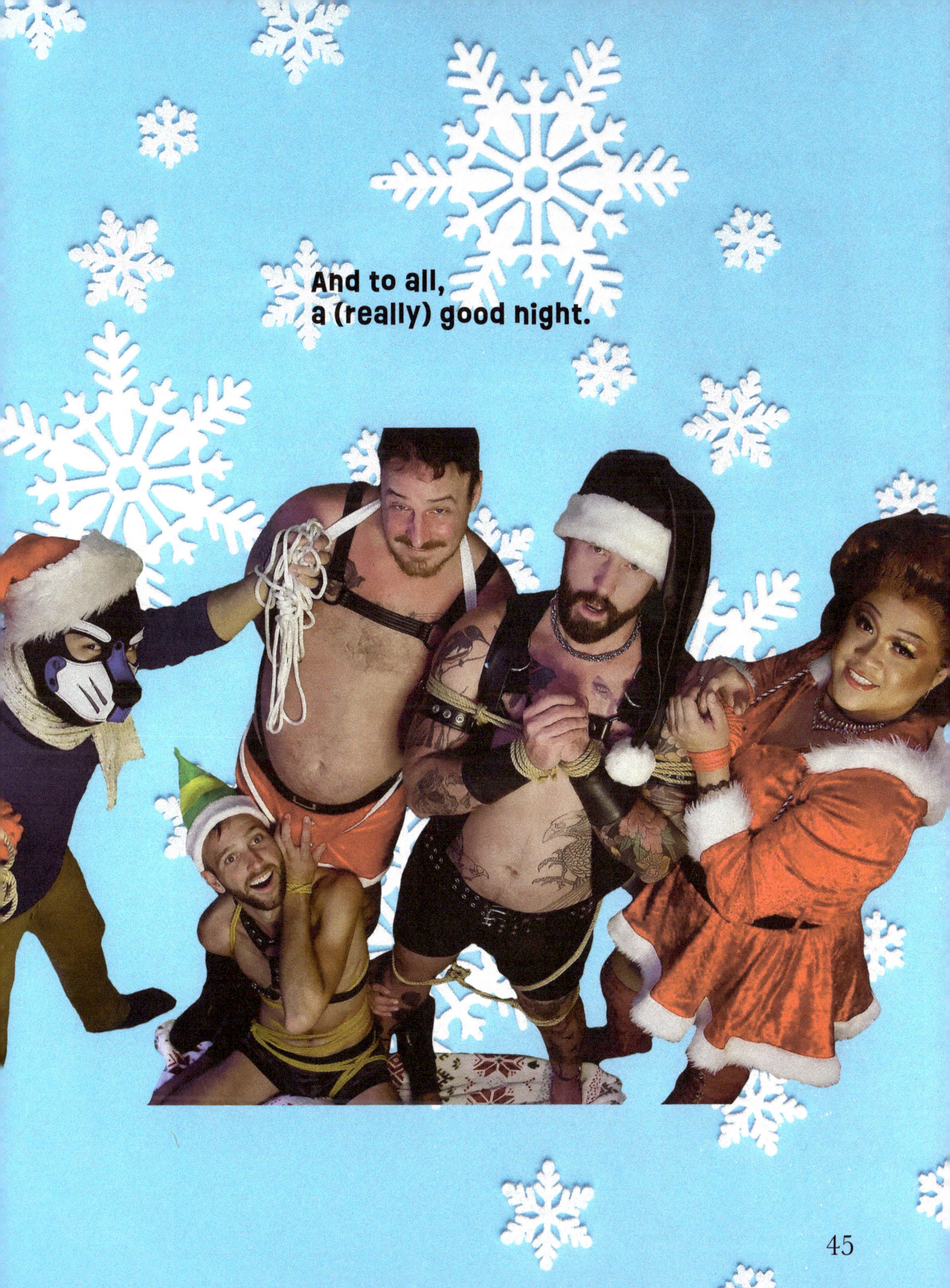
And to all,
a (really) good night.

The Naughty List Gallery

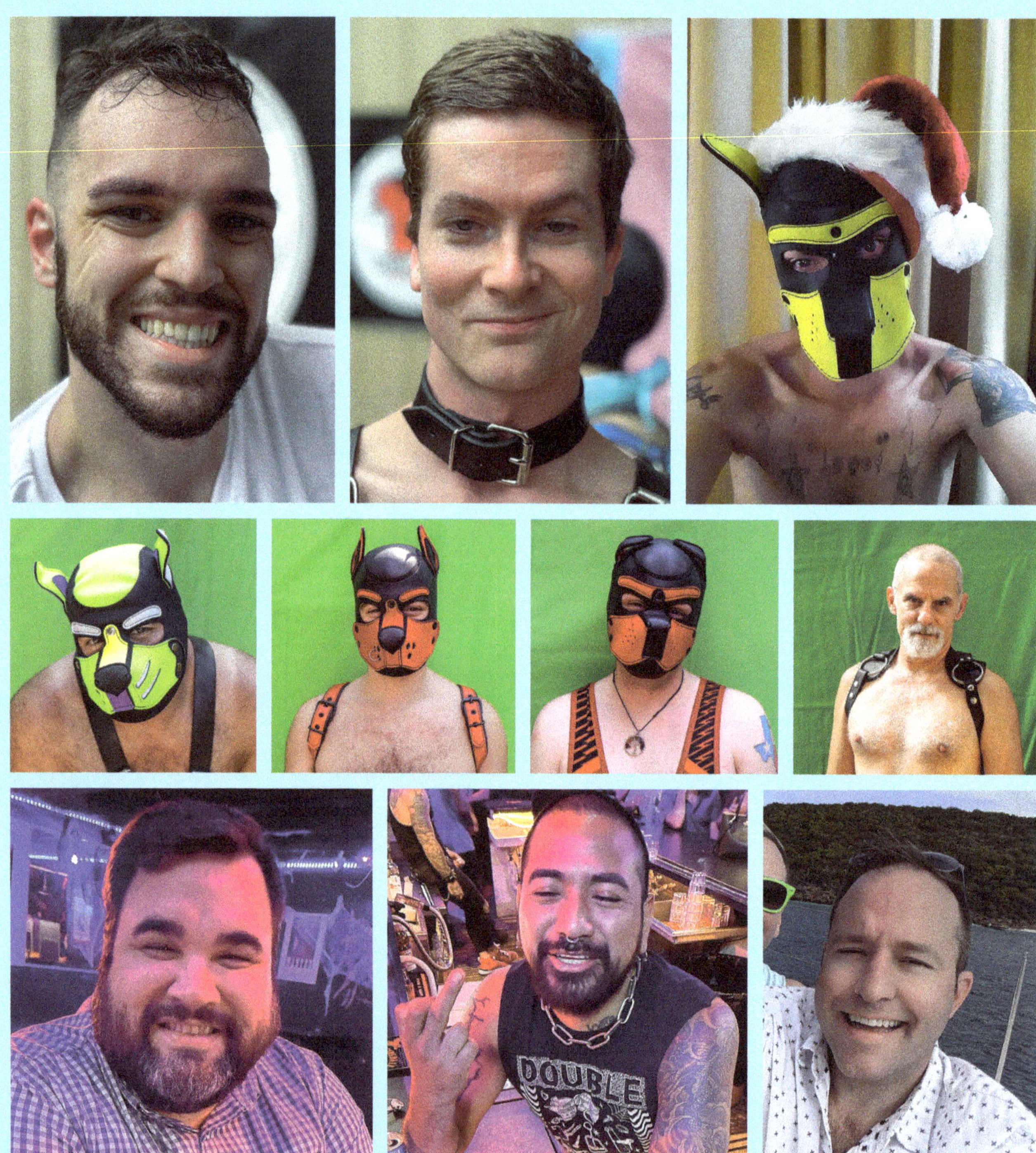

The Naughty List Gallery

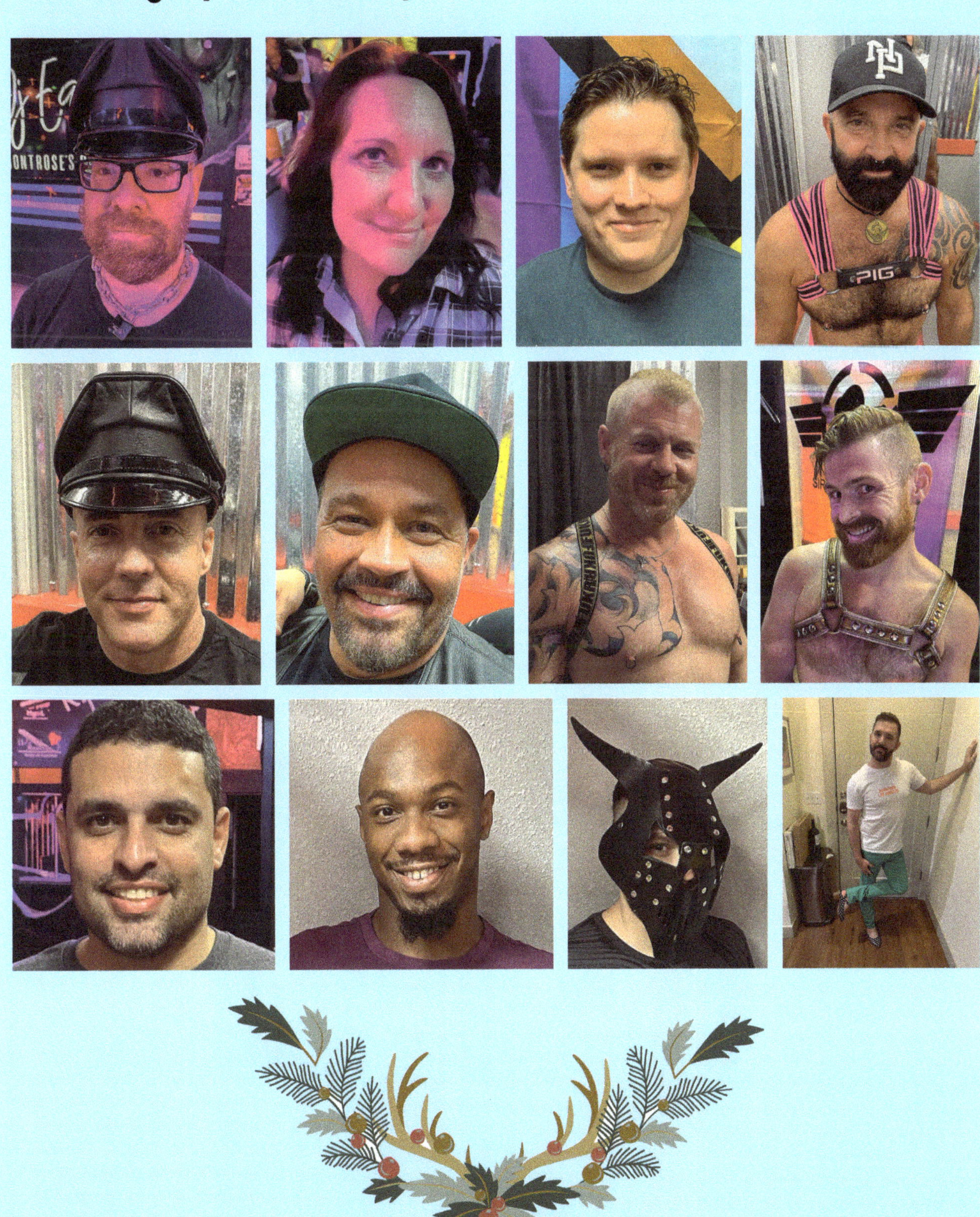

The Naughty List Gallery

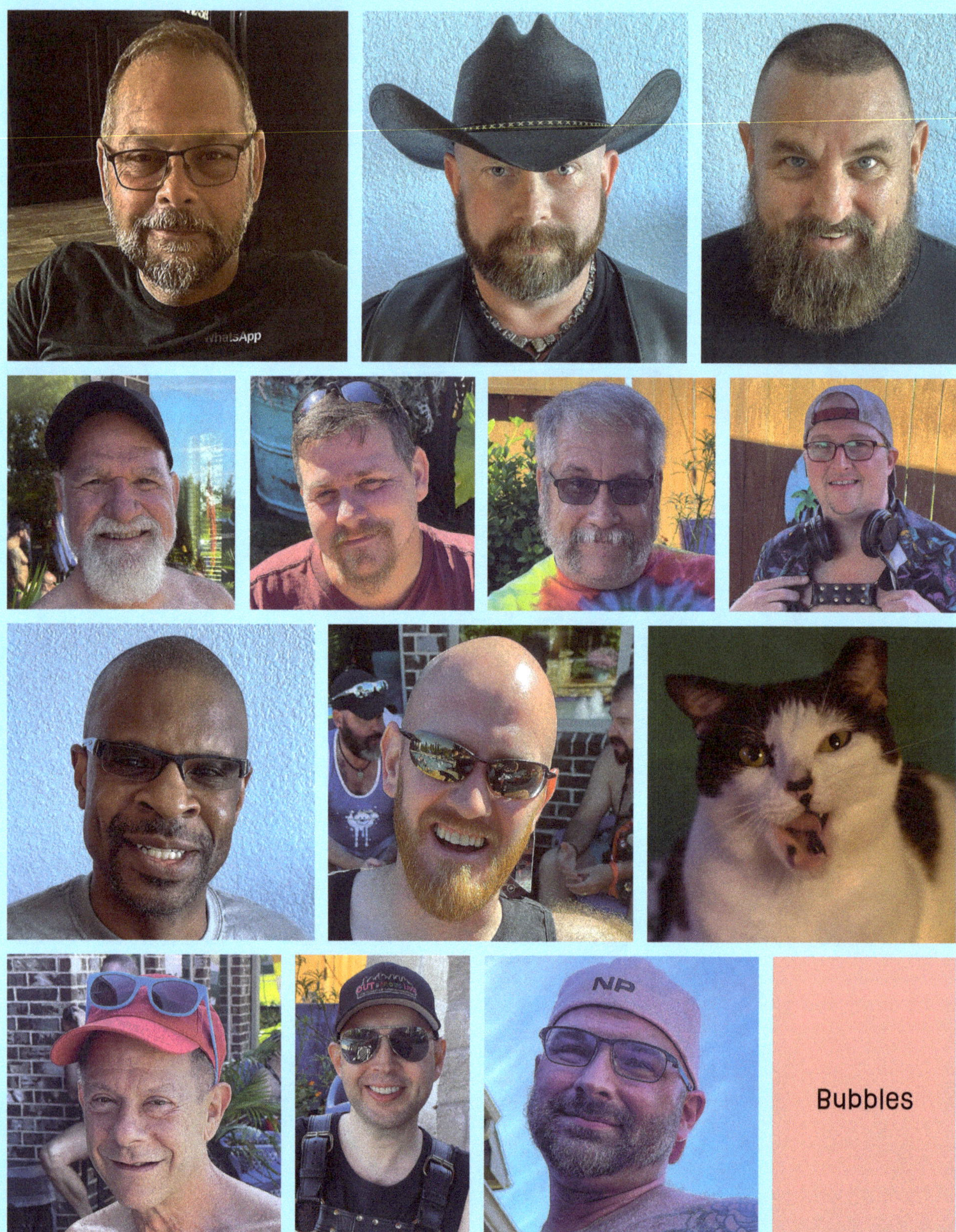

The Naughty List Gallery

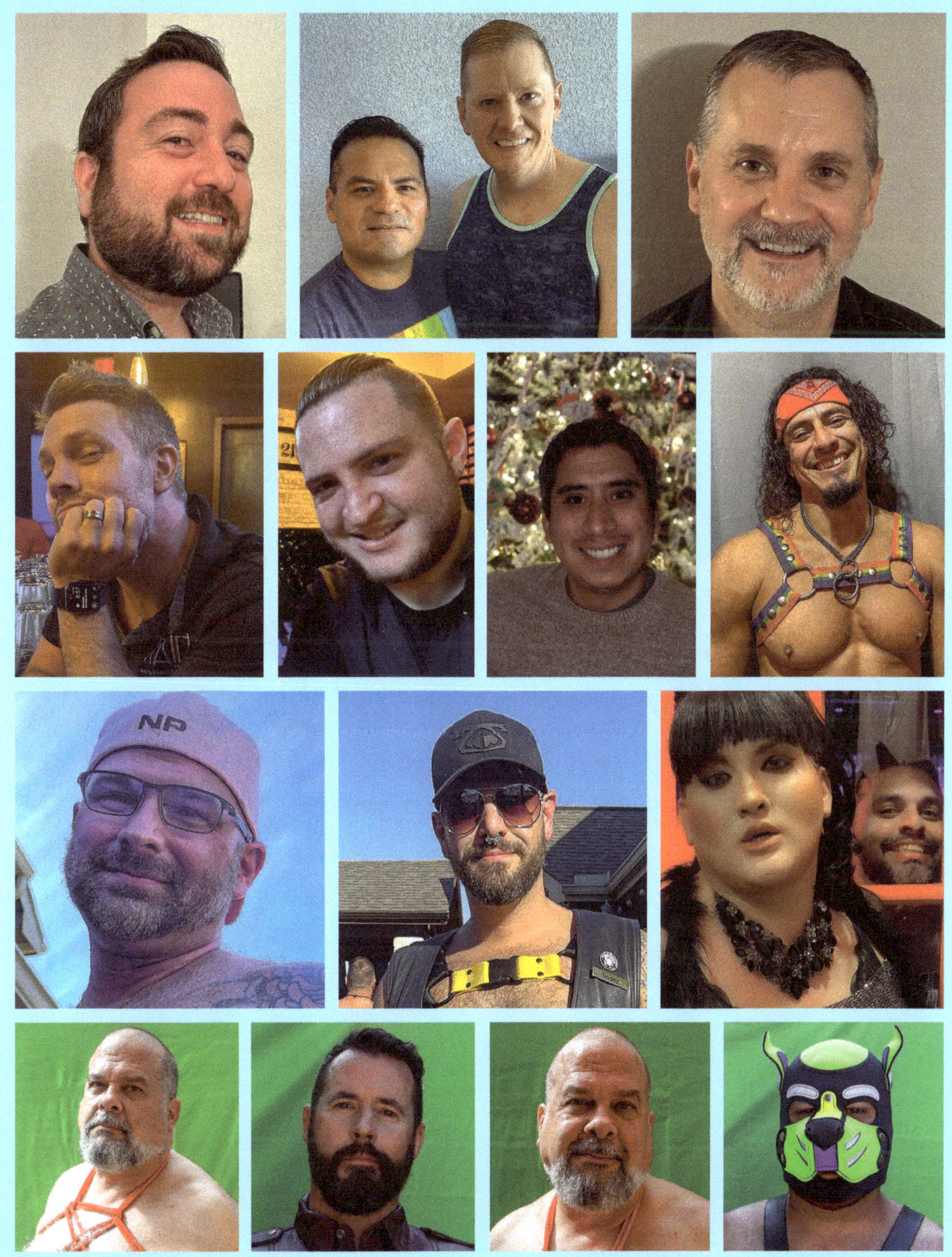

The Naughty List Gallery

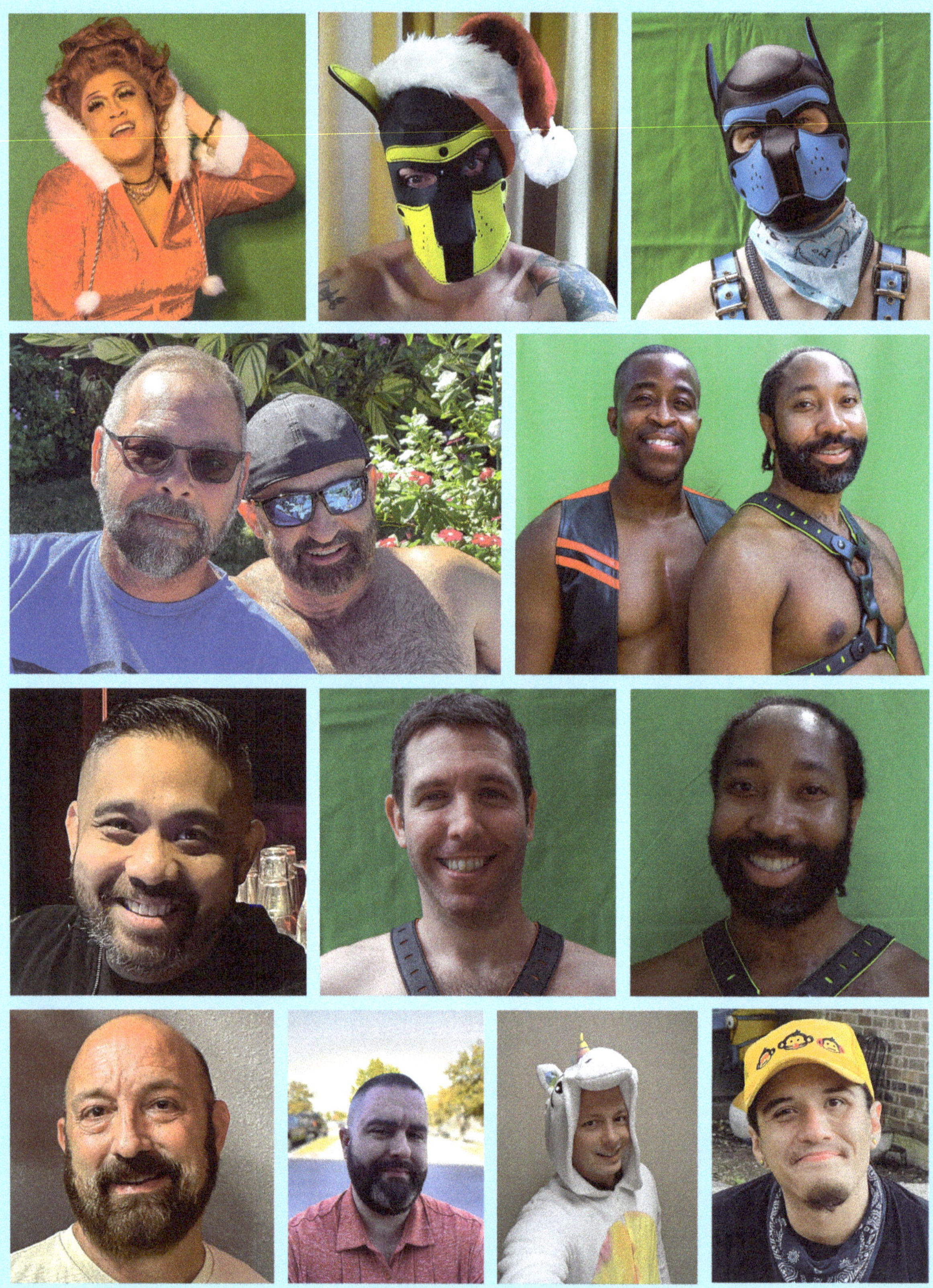

Encore

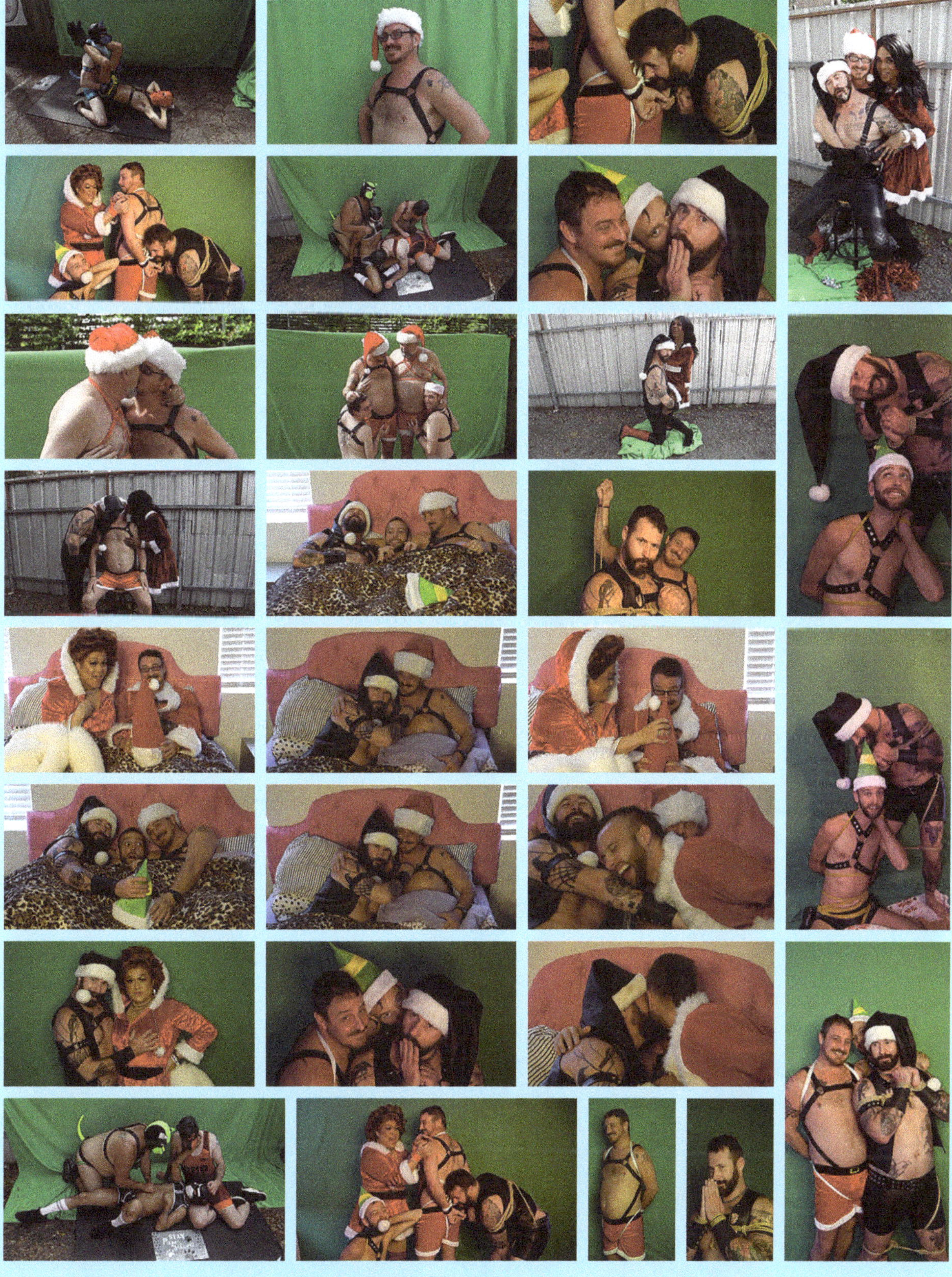

Good night.

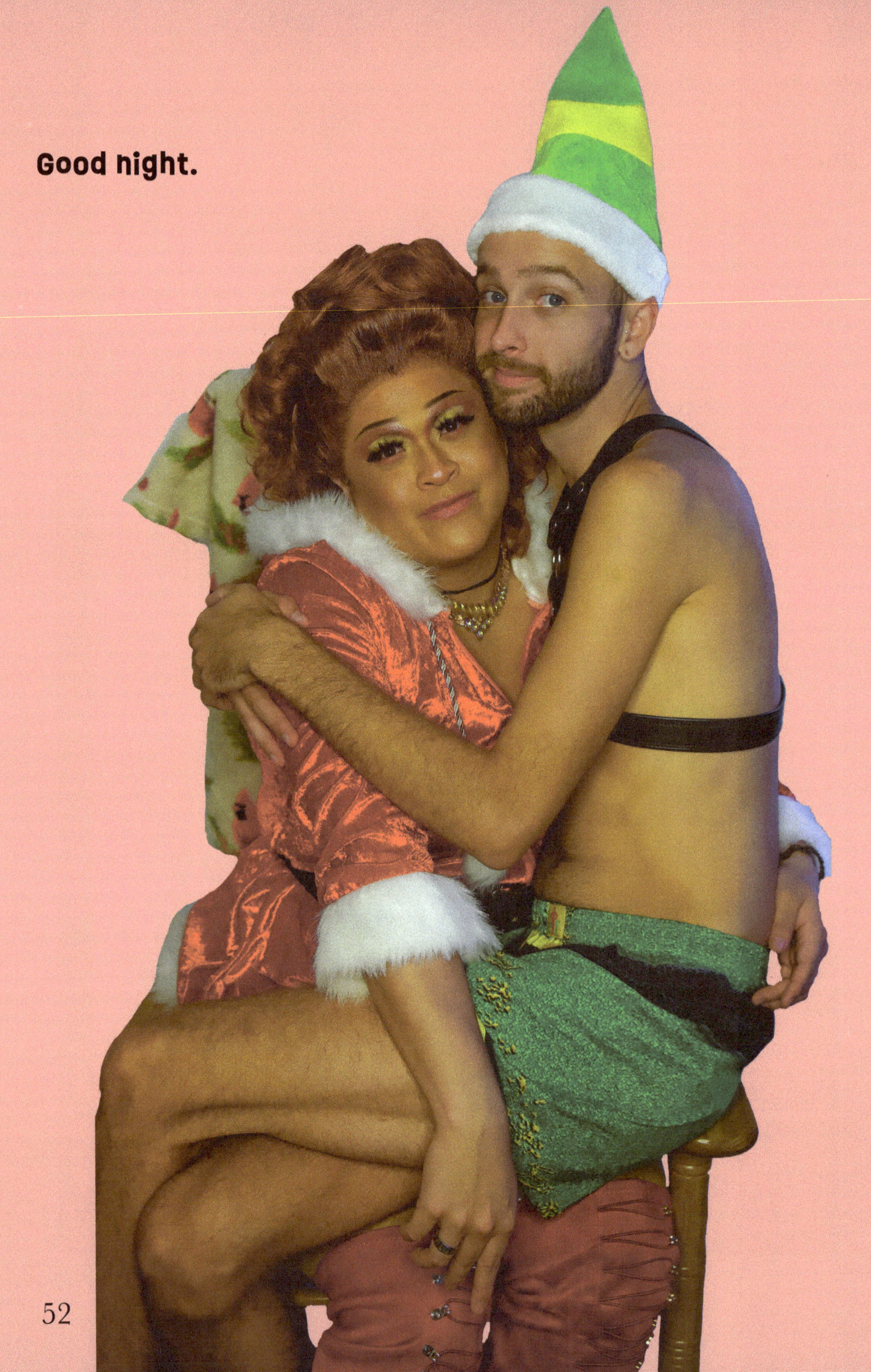

www.ingramcontent.com/pod-product-compliance
Lightning Source LLC
LaVergne TN
LVHW060643110826
845147LV00018B/1029
9798985173901